Skrifter utgivna vid Juridiska fakulteten i Lund
Nr 169
Acta Societatis Juridicae Lundensis

Skrifter utgivna vid Juridiska fakulteten i Lund
Nr 169
Acta Societatis Juridicae Lundensis

Globalization and the U. S. Law School

Comparative and Cultural Perspectives

1906–2006

Juristförlaget i Lund
Distribution: eddy.se

Editors
Stephen C. Hicks, Kjell Å. Modéer

This book demonstrates the constructive and increased interaction and cooperation between the Faculty of Law at Lund University and Suffolk University Law School in Boston. In 2009 is also celebrated ten years of transatlantic cooperation between law students and law professors at these two law schools. Viveat, floreat, crescat!

Address for orders: eddy.se AB
Bookorder
Box 1310
S-621 24 Visby
+46 (0)498 253900 (tel)
+46 (0)498 249789 (fax)

Publisher's address: Juristförlaget i Lund
Box 207
221 00 Lund
+46 (0)46 222 10 09 (tel)
www.juristforlaget.se

ISBN 978-91-544-0111-6

Grafisk form: *Alf Dahlberg*/PAN EIDOS
Layout: HANS-HEINRICH VOGEL
Tryck: Wallin &Dalholm Boktryckeri AB
Lund 2009
ISBN 978–91–544–0111–6
ISSN 1402–4276 (Skrifter utgivna vid Juridiska fakulteten i Lund)

Table of Contents

Preface

International agreements between universities or faculties are never stronger than the personal relations between their individuals. And even establishing of networks between individual scholars is easier to create than to build up an institutional mutual cooperation. In that respect it's impressive to observe how the cooperation between Suffolk University Law School in Boston Massachusetts and the Faculty of Law at Lund University in Sweden has developed from scratch to a well-operated cooperation in several fields in about 10 years. Mutual relationships have been established between scholars on both sides of the Atlantic Ocean; scholars have visited the other law school for a shorter or longer period, a couple of them have also served as visiting teachers; a summer-school at Lund with students from both Suffolk and Lund is operating since 1998; many master students and several Lund ph.d. students have spent semesters at Suffolk, and also within the Lund-Vietnamese *law and development*-project the Suffolk staff has been involved in a meaningful and constructive way. The whole operation has developed in mutual trust in the need for an international orientated law school in our challenging time of globalization. In that respect the Lund—Suffolk program is demonstrating how successful such an international enterprise can develop—thanks to individual relations.

Even more interesting and successful is the intellectual interaction which has developed between the scholars involved. It can to a great extent be identified as an enterprise within comparative law. During the last decade the discourses within the discipline of comparative law has increased dramatically. They have transformed the field of comparative law from a traditional functional discipline into a contextual one, using concepts like history, culture and tradition as important parameters in our current time of dichotomies: transparency vs. closed borders, free movements and open boundaries vs. national security, tolerance and respect vs. intolerance and fundamentalism, and Eurocentricity and parochial narcissism vs. trans-national activities together with the diversity of non Western countries. In sum: national black letter law vs. contextual legal constructs. All of them are high priority discourses of great value not only for the academic and scholarly environment of law but also for each law student preparing for practice in a multicultural and multi-religious post September 11-world.

To take it from the very beginning: The starting point for the symposium presented in this volume was the class of *comparative legal cultures* Steve Hicks and I co-taught at Lund in the summer-school of 2002. The material we used in the class was the then newly published book *Legal Traditions of the World* by our common Canadian friend and colleague H. Patrick Glenn at McGill University. Not only the concept of oral tradition used in this book was a challenging and provoking approach, also the courage of the author to write a one volume book on his interpretation of this global topic was impressive. We learnt a lot during this course, perhaps both of us more than the students did.

Since then we have co-taught classes both at Lund and Suffolk and we have cooperated in arranging an international comparative law seminar—together with e.g. Patrick Glenn—at the Hanoi Law University in 2006. We have both nuanced our scholarly positions thanks to the participation in these discourses. I think it's fair to state that our cooperation demonstrates the importance of using comparative law in the law school in our time of globalization.

When Suffolk Law School planned its centenary in 2006 it was evident that the Lund Law School should be included in its celebrations. We took the initiative to a bi-partial celebration with a symposium co-arranged between Suffolk and Lund. We wanted this symposium to be contribution to our commitment to the comparative law and to the discourses on legal cultures and on the legal history of the 20th century, *Law's Century*.

Taking legal education as the main theme for the symposium was related to the current discourse on the legal profession as the indicator of national legal cultures. Pierre Legrand in his epistemological concept of comparative legal culture emphasizes the importance of legal education and legal training for the differences within European legal systems. Due to these differences European legal systems are not converging. In the United States Robert Stevens' today classical work on the *Law School: Legal Education in America from the 1850's to the 1980's* gave the broad overview to the American development, and in the U.K. William Twining's book *Blackstone's Tower: The English Law School* (1994) described a historical perspective.[1] Since the early 1990's the legal education has changed dramatically—in the U.S. as well as in Sweden. It not only has been internationalized—in the U.S. also nationalized—it also has got much more of interdisciplinarity in form of *law ands*. The current works on

[1] Robert Stevens, Law School: Legal Education in America from 1850's to the 1980's. Chapel Hill: University of North Carolina Press 1993.

the Yale Law School by Laura Kalman[2] and Anthony Kronman[3] are confirming this new interest for the historical, comparative and interdisciplinary approaches to the study of the legal education and the Law School.

So it became evident that the most natural theme for the symposium was to devote it to the legal education at our two institutions during the past century and it should give its participants insights not only about the changes in contexts and applications but also about the sustainability and the enduring traditions within legal knowledge and legal communication, as well as to the theoretical and pragmatic approaches to the law. The symposium was orchestrated as a comparative drama in three parts. The first scene was set in 1906 telling about Suffolk and Lund at the time for the foundation of the Suffolk Law School. The second was set about 1950 and the peak of the time of legal realism and law in action, and the third set concerned the current legal education. To this concluding part of the symposium U.S. Supreme Court Justice Ruth Bader Ginsburg—holding an honorary degree from the Lund University Law Faculty—gave a brilliant address and participated in a lively and discursive conversation with the then Suffolk Dean Robert Smitt and me, Kjell Å. Modéer. Justice Ginsburg's address is included is this volume.

We want to thank the participating colleagues for offering their papers to this centennial volume and we also want to thank *Juristförlaget i Lund* for publishing the papers from this memorable event.

Lund and Boston, January 2008.

Kjell Å. Modéer *Stephen C. Hicks*

---

[2] Laura Kalman, Yale Law School and the Sixties: Revolt and Reverberations, Univ. of North Carolina Press: Chapel Hill 2009.

[3] Anthony T. Kronman (ed.), History of the Yale Law School, Yale University Press: New Haven 2004.

Stephen C. Hicks

Introduction

The papers, essays and articles in this book are the product of a ten year collaboration, a friendship of nearly forty years, and one hundred years of the evolution of legal education.

The Conference at which they were presented celebrated the Centennial of the founding of Suffolk Law School, as it was then, at which Supreme Court Justice Ruth Bader Ginsburg was the keynote speaker, a long time friend of Professor Kjell Å. Modéer of Lund University's law faculty, with which Suffolk University Law School has had a multi-faceted and productive collaboration for the last ten years.

The papers cover a lot of ground, but have some common themes, among them one in particular, the question raised by Jack Schlegel, whether "we are all realists now" because of the internationalization of legal education, the globalization of the world's economies, and the resulting transformation of the study of law into a more practical and less theoretical discipline. This is law as action, not talk or reflection, but the business of law as a business today in which lawyers need to know what others are doing all over the world. Realistically then, law is about problem solving, which requires cross cultural understanding, comparative knowledge and the perspective of historical change to make sense of it all. Whether or not this is what the Legal Realists meant, or whether it makes us all "realists now" is for the reader to consider. Of course, the authors take different positions on this.

Central to the discussion is the history of Suffolk Law School as it evolved through "law's century." It is the different dimensions to the law's century that give coherence to the papers; in an abstract sense, there is the contrast of theory and practice, but there is also the contrast of the common law and the civil law, the U.S. and Europe, and the very real contrast of learning the law as an apprentice, at a professional trade school, or in a university. The authors here take such geographical, historical and professional dimensions as given, in exploring the different ways "law's century" has led us to the first decade of the 21st century, in which, despite the challenges we face to remain true to an original vision of law and legal education, Jack Schlegel can claim legal realism is still the "soul" of American law.

At the Conference, speakers described law's century as one of the rise of American law, especially in the context of globalization today. But others demurred, describing it as partial, unequal and regressive, or from a grander perspective, as imperialistic, and bemoaning the fact that the rest of the world is poised to adopt the worst aspects of the U.S. legal education system. But whether the Central European and Eurasian Law Initiative of the 90' is a failure, because the Rule of Law is misunderstood abroad, or we overlook the importance of human rights when we talk about trade, because of our parochial concerns, the fact is that exports and transplants do not always take root. This too is for the reader to consider.

The story begins in a small apartment in Boston in 1906. Gleason Archer used his initiative and ambition to found a law school for immigrants without a high school education or a college degree, in defiance of the social elite, the political establishment, and the legal profession. In Mike Rustad's memorable phrase, this was "opportunity's open door." To use Weber's word, Archer tried to demystify legal education, by not using the case method, by having frequent tests and strict standards, that is, in a phrase, by adopting a practical approach to the law. It also initiated a change in the profession from an aristocratic calling to a democratic task.

The continuous struggle for a small and new institution to survive and to become recognized as legitimate is well told by Rustad; it is a real Horatio Alger morality play. On the one hand, money and power resisted any alternative to their sponsored innovations. On the other hand, the case method was criticized as much as it was observed, by none other than Jerome Frank, for example, who used it as a foil for his more realistic approach to learning the law, by which he meant, in a clinical setting. Suffolk did not represent that at all. But nonetheless, the link between legal realism and Suffolk is there, albeit a link forged of different ideals. That is, realism as practical active learning not case law, and realism as skills not theory.

In fact, however, Archer's ideals have been betrayed, in that Suffolk has since been "Harvardized" by adopting the case method, funding law reviews, relying on teaching by professional scholars, and presenting a big and impressive library to the world. Rustad argues that this is not the point. The point is that today the "night school" is the chosen professional path of many young Ph.D.'s whom Harvard would delight in having in its classes, but who are still looking for the open door of opportunity and finding it closed by a classical version of legal education. This is indeed the measure of Suffolk's success that Rustad urges us to recognize. We are successful at what we do, and what we do best is still consistent with our past even as we adapt it to the present. Those seeking opportunity today are patent agents, for example.On the other hand, as Bruce Smith points out, it could be said to have come full circle now after a hundred years, since the case method has lost out to a more practice based model for the training of lawyers. It is not just that Suffolk followed a predictable trajectory, from being an outsider and a rebel, to compromising and then joining the club, the American Association of Law Schools, and finally claiming its rightful market share, at first local but increasingly national. Suffolk mirrored many other developments in the first half of the twentieth century. Suffolk's lawyers became businessmen as well as professionals. The creation of law schools separate from universities restated in a new form the role of the lawyer as agent of justice, not so much as statesman. Although Suffolk was successful in filling the ranks of the local judiciary and state house, its rank and file missionaries were simple counsel for the underprivileged. With opening the door to the poor came the service to the working classes that fuelled much of the success of Suffolk lawyers, as politicians and as practitioners. This was consistent with the liberal and progressive nature of the times. At the same time, Suffolk experienced the kind of ambivalence seen by legal realism, between the need to learn the skills of analysis and reasoning, and the need for exposure to the processes of the law, the one seen originally as theoretical, and the other as practical; but of course, today, they are both seen as involving the class room and the office. In this too, Suffolk reflected the swings of the pendulum from a narrow and basic curriculum to a smorgasbord of electives, as much as it constituted its own image as the school of opportunity.

Much more can be seen from a comparative perspective, however, of the ways Suffolk was also consistent with developments in at least one other part of the world. Although there were other such entrepreneurial endeavors, even in Boston, if one thinks of Suffolk with its night school as a metropolitan place of learning, as opposed to the classical universities like Harvard, then there are historical parallels with Sweden. At just about the same time, 1906, there occurred in Sweden a similar reaction to the inadequacy of studying just the law in books, and it led to the creation of a metropolitan law school at Stockholm, in reaction to the traditional learning at Lund and Uppsala. Although the context of this change is different, since Swedish lawyers were trained to become civil servants not private practitioners, and the law was civil not common law, yet the similarities are both on the surface, by aiming to modernize the profession and legal education, and also deeper, in that Sweden and Harvard drew upon German ideas of educational theory. Modéer's detailed unraveling of this history is rarely explained in English. His essay is a wonderful contribution to our understanding of modernization and its forces of change at the turn of the nineteenth century both in the U.S. and in Sweden, through a "Germanization," not unlike our "Harvardization," though not merely institutional, but a more pervasive cultural and authoritative phenomenon.

It is this unity, although a simplification, of historical context, as the reality that we always find ourselves in, that Jack Schlegel takes as his text for analyzing the parallel developments of theory and practice. As Rustad reminds us of the importance of practice to education, so does Modéer argue that we cannot ignore theory and history. Schlegel puts it this way: legal education reflected legal theory and vice versa, such that the "soul" of American law transmigrates from one to the other, in turns, as legal realism in theory and education, and realism in practice and theory, and realism in education and practice.

As we see the evolution of legal theory from formalism to sociological jurisprudence to legal realism to the school of legal process, and even critical legal studies, we also see the transition from rules to behavior to institutions and clinics and power as objects of study, which are simultaneously made manifest in education and legal practice by being understood empirically. Schlegel's exposition of legal realism, both as a mid century phenomenon and as the continuous thread of the legal reality that we professors, theorists and practitioners face, is in part familiar but also very instructive and original. He describes, as only someone thoroughly immersed in his subject can, legal science as professional craft. In great detail, he shows how empiricism has been manifested in the study of rules in the library, the judicial process and the practice of law, and how the logical, psychological and sociological critiques have led to new courses, programs and policies. Empiricism is the soul of American law which has transmigrated to different bodies throughout the twentieth century. Schlegel ends with a very positive description of a course he teaches which exemplifies his own high standards and his own ideals with regard to realism in theory, education and practice. But few of us are realists in that sense today, or aspire to it even, as he laments. Smith suggests this may be a little pessimistic in his comments on the speakers. Empiricism is not out of favor, it too has been transformed.

It might be said that the transmigration of the soul of law today is now in search of another body to inhabit. Schlegel's fear is that it might be what he calls "normative theorizing," which was critiqued by panelists whose contributions are not in this volume, for its lack of openness, limited access, inequality and loss of idealism, as well as obviously its lack of realism and empiricism.

Perhaps that "body" however, is comparative law, as the medium of globalization and internationalization. Mathias Reimann takes "trans-migration" more literally. At he same time as legal realism was taking root, the first émigré refugees were coming to the U.S. bringing the reality of different legal systems and pedagogies to the U.S. Interestingly enough though, Reimann will conclude similarly that everyone knows how important these foreign scholars of foreign law were, (read: legal realism) but in fact they came to so little (read: legal realism, per Schlegel).

His survey covers the second half of the twentieth century which was marked by three different incursions of transmigrating lawyers and scholars. Only recently might one say that the soul of American law has inhabited the body of comparative law, and even then one must make allowances for its contradiction and subversiveness in the eyes of some. In his essay one can also see the deep connections between legal realism, émigré professors and Germany. Germany figures in his story very differently from that of Modéer; not as the late nineteenth century source of new ideas about education, but as the twentieth century force from which refugees fled. Also, the learning from books in the library, as in the case method, was resisted by legal realism, and reinforced by scholars who really did flee a real legal system which was really perverted by Nazi law. Their realism was different from that of the early realists, just as the later émigrés differed from the later ones.

Of course one can say that the new international scholars brought with them the comparative methodology. But in fact this was not influential because their substantive areas of private law were less interesting to academics than public law, their value of knowledge for knowledge's sake led to grand overviews not useful doctrinal analysis, and quite simply Europe and the civil law system were suspect after the second world war. But Reimann suggests that current scholarship shows that the émigrés from Germany initiated the breakdown of the parochialism of American scholarship and engendered a receptiveness to transnational and global perspectives.

A new generation of younger scholars came to the U.S. in the sixties and seventies, myself included, for different reasons than the first wave of refugees. We were explorers of an optimistic, new world order, intellectual travelers from all corners of the globe drawn to the U.S. for its freedom of opportunity and its anticipated contribution to global change: immigrants yes, but also less concerned with fitting in, and more concerned with what we could get out of the experience of legal education and legal practice abroad. This meant a different approach to the comparative study of law, more international and less domestic, more political and cultural and less theoretical, more procedural and practical and less doctrinal.

New courses and their progeny of articles and books began to appear like "Comparative Legal Systems", "Chinese Law and Ideology" and "Comparative Criminal Procedure". Nevertheless, speaking from experience, such curriculum developments and scholarship were still viewed with skepticism. It has only been recently that the inspiration behind this has not been marginalized and has become mainstream, in the form of Global Trade Law or something like International Business Transactions. Comparative law is of course the key to this new realism of law in action. It does have its detractors. But no one can argue with the sheer numbers of students, scholars, programs, exchanges, agreements, joint projects, migrating around the world, across borders, representing a dramatic shift in legal education from the domestic horizon to the global. Suffolk and Lund are actors in the internationalization of legal education which is reflective of the internationalization of legal practice.

So much may seem obvious. Reimann ends with some observations though, which should caution the reader to jumping to conclusions. A lot of this has been one-way traffic, the export of U.S. law and the import of international students. The internationalization of legal education has increased the U.S.'s sense of self importance. Comparative law has been very Eurocentric in the U.S. and not really global. We do not see the vast resources we have in the U.S. of first and second generation immigrants who will play an increasingly important role in world affairs and who are a domestic supply of international lawyers because of their language, cultural and legal skills. But at the same time, Europe also has been very narrowly western in its orientation, until recently. Reimann's paper is part of his wider scholarship on comparative law in the twentieth century and he is well able to pull together such disparate observations.

This big picture is narrowed by the final paper here, that of Thomas Lundmark, to the singular case of Germany, seen now not as the nineteenth century source of much that was right and wrong in American law in the early twentieth century, or the source of the transmigration of scholars who brought a different kind of realism to America in the middle of the twentieth century, but the Germany which is one of the world's strongest economies, yet clings to an outdated mode of legal education, ill preparing its brightest young minds for law in the twenty first century.

Lundmark's description of the forces of tradition and change in modern

German legal education gives revealing insight into the classical university system in another country. Again, these details are not easy to find in the English literature. His perspective is unique too, as an American professor of the Common Law at a German law faculty. Being versed in legal theory too, he explains that the tension is the same, between the law in the books and the law in action, so that it is a German form of legal realism that challenges the status quo to adapt to modern demands of the global economy. The modern lawyer is trained to be a problem solver, not to assume the mantle of the lawyer as civil servant. Here is an echo of a major theme throughout the book, bringing together Suffolk, Sweden and Legal Realism. Lundmark cross references other themes too, such as, the parochialism of national pride, the free market of ideas and their transformation when they take root somewhere else.

Most importantly, as we reflect on Suffolk's Centennial and its cooperation with Lund, the opinion was expressed that the U.S. only gets "Global Realism" now because there are competitors for the provision of legal services, legal education and legal theory to the rest of the world. This cynical charge is akin to the notion that globalization is really only a front for "Americanization", and is repeated in many of the critiques of the influence of the American model of professional legal education, upon the rest of the world. This is laid at the feet of legal realism, for separating learning the law's doctrine from the classical curriculum of history, philosophy and literature. Putting aside the case-method and problem solving, two different sides of what we now think of as the same coin, this is exactly how Legal Realism is seen today. It is in this sense that we are all realists now.

Nevertheless, realism is evolving and adapting, as does everything. It has transmigrated into the cultural relativity of global homogeneity, a paradox reconcilable only by thinking of legal education as the same everywhere, striving to service the same business interests, and thinking of the law being similarly transnational, but yet dependent on the local environment. The Bologna Protocol and the Erasmus Program exemplify just this, the latter providing study abroad and transfer of credits across Europe, and the former harmonizing the credit system, the transcripts, the programmatic requirements of legal education, and even the professional qualifications of lawyers. Ironically, says Lundmark, Germany has successfully resisted this normalization, even though its legal education may need an overhaul in the eyes of its consumers.

But here is where the issue lies, just beneath the surface of the influence of realism. It is not clear even to Americans today that post-graduate law schools, of three years duration, aimed at preparation for a single exam for admission to the bar, without any internship, clinical training or apprenticeship is a satisfactory way to train professionals.As the essays demonstrate in this volume, and as Smith argues in his essay, the history of the last one hundred years of U.S. legal education cannot be uncritically acclaimed, any more than the mythic trajectory of humble beginnings leading to modern success can be taken at face value.

The U.S. model demands that its graduates are able to "hit the ground running." This puts pressure on law schools to do everything in their graduate degree, from theory, to history, to doctrine and skills, and bar exam preparation. Suffolk's mythic self image still expresses Archer's claim that our students are prepared to practice law. But the obverse question to whether the rest of the world really should believe that, is whether our U.S. law graduates are ready to practice law on a global scale, when most international lawyers speak at least two languages and have studied abroad. Reimann may be close to the truth in saying that the soul of realism has transmigrated to "comparative law" and it is no longer embodied in U.S. law.

Acknowledgements

We want to acknowledge the support and assistance of both our Universities and Law Schools, and friends and colleagues, in particular:

Suffolk University President David Sargent
Patricia Meservey, Provost, Suffolk University
Dean Robert Smith, Suffolk University Law School
Associate Dean John Deliso
Associate Dean Marc Perlin
Associate Dean Bernard Keenan
Bridgett Halay, Director of International and Graduate Programs
Professor Bernard Ortwein
Professor Christopher Gibson
Professor Valerie Epps
Professor Marie Ashe
Paula Higgins-Baker, Administrative Assistant
Helen Lynch, Staff Assistant
George Comeau, Managing Associate Director, University Media Services
Brian McDermott, Assistant Director, University Media Services
Patricia Gallagher, Event Coordinator
James Barrett, Webmaster, Academic Technology
Kara Peterson, Director, Communications
Professor Martha Chamallas, Moritz College of Law, Ohio State University
Professor David Hall, Northeastern School of Law, Boston
Carl Monk, Executive Vice-President, American Association of Law Schools
Margaret Marshall, Chief Justice, Massachusetts Supreme Judicial Court

Ruth Bader Ginsburg[*]

Remarks to Suffolk

When Dean Smith and Kjell Modéer asked me to participate in this celebration I said yes without hesitation. This is only my second visit to Suffolk Law School, the first was in the late 1970s, many years before most people in this audience were born. The school had assembled a stellar crew of lawyers to speak on appellate advocacy. Not yet a judge, I had been actively engaged in that form of advocacy as one of the ACLU's General Counsel and co-founder of the Union's Women's Rights Project. For the conference at Suffolk, I stepped back to think and write about what I strived to accomplish in briefs and oral argument. I recycled that talk many times for CLE programs during my years on the D.C. Circuit.

My affiliation with Lund University has deeper roots. I spent several months in Sweden in 1962 and 1963, attempting to learn about, and then convey to a common-law bar and bench, the main lines of Sweden's judicial system. My base was Lund, where my co-author, Anders Bruzelius, lived and served as a city court judge. In those years I came to appreciate the value of a comparative perspective on the law. An unexpected dividend. Studying about and observing another legal system in operation, I came to understand more completely the United States system in which I was schooled. I became a better teacher of procedure and a better judge, too, I believe, as a result of the experience.

The good job I now hold attracts honors and honorary degrees by the score. But no honor I have ever received has pleased me more than the honorary degree Lund University awarded to me and my co-author in 1969. I was given a tall pleated hat with a brass buckle at that promotion ceremony, and a finely crafted gold ring. The hat accounts for my popularity as a graduation speaker, and the ring is the only ring I have worn constantly from that day to this.

The topic of this conference is legal education as it has developed here and abroad. Before we begin our conversation I thought it appropriate to comment briefly on contributions of two kinds law faculties are equipped to make to the health and welfare of our legal system.

My first observation concerns the aid academicians can give to judges. As

---

* Associate Justice, Supreme Court of the United States

a judge now for some 26 years, I appreciate the importance of academic commentary. Our legal system gives judges considerable authority to shape the law through litigated cases. We entrust that large authority mainly to generalists, to jurists who cannot do their job well without help from specialists in the academy.

Benjamin Cardozo expressed the point best: "The Judge goes upon the Bench, and sees before him a list of names and numbers … [O]ne case follows another. … More and more in such cases we are driven . . . to rely upon the work of a [legal scholar] … It is not to be expected … that overnight and at the call of a single case we shall do the work … [scholars] have been doing in lifetimes of devoted and intensive effort."

At the Supreme Court in recent terms, the number of law professor amici briefs we have received has notably increased. I count that a good and useful development. Several of the best oral advocates appearing before the Court nowadays, I might add, are law teachers.

Faculty members can similarly inform lawmakers in legislative chambers and practitioners of the law. And they can advance popular understanding and public dialogue through contributions to broadcast and print media.

My second observation concerns the public spirit law schools should strive to foster among law students. Law has been called a learned profession. That label will be undeserved if lawyers are trained simply to become skilled artisans, ready, willing, and able to earn fees for their craft.

Law and lawyers, one cannot avoid acknowledging, have fared rather badly in many a song and story. In grand opera, for example, lawyers are barely there. In Johann Strauss's Die Fledermaus, a lawyer has a bit part, but his assistance is so ineffective, he manages to get his client a few extra days in jail. The lawyer in Porgy and Bess ups the price to get Bess a divorce when she tells him she was never really married before.

Celebrated writers from Shakespeare to Sandburg have harbored a lingering distrust of the lawyers' trade. Charles Dickens, in Bleak House, put it this way:

The one great principle of the English law is to make business for itself. There is no other principle so distinctly, certainly, and consistently maintained through all its narrow turnings. Viewed by this light it becomes a coherent scheme and not the monstrous maze the laity are apt to think it. Let them but once clearly perceive that its grand principle is to make business for itself at their expense, and surely they will cease to grumble.

But the legal profession has among its practitioners brave men and women who strive to change that perception, jurists devoted to, and at work for, the public good—people who are the best of lawyers and judges, the most dedicated, the least selfish. Law faculties should seek to train lawyers fitting that description, young men and women who will regard the practice of law as a public calling.

It is time now to invite your questions. One ground rule: I cannot respond to a question aimed to uncover how the Court will rule in a pending case or might rule in a matter likely to come before the Court. That is the sum and substance of what some reporters dubbed "the Ginsburg rule" in recent confirmation hearings.

MICHAEL L. RUSTAD[1]

A HARD DAY'S NIGHT: THE HIDDEN HISTORY OF HOW SUFFOLK LAW SCHOOL HELPED TO DIVERSIFY AMERICAN LEGAL EDUCATION[2]

"Some are born to sweet delight.
Some are born to endless night."[3]
William Blake

Introduction

By the first decade of the twentieth century, there were two competing routes to becoming a lawyer in Massachusetts that were as different as day and night. From 1890 to 1914, as evening law schools sprouted up in every major city, the number of law students increased five times.[4] During the early twentieth century, the evening school movement contributed to the American legal profession's, transformation from patrician to a professional field. The night law schools reflected a counter hegemonic movement in legal education to

[1] Michael L. Rustad, Ph.D., J.D., LL.M. is the Thomas F. Lambert Jr. Professor of Law and Co-Director of the Intellectual Property Law Concentration at Suffolk University Law School in Boston, Massachusetts.

[2] This chapter is based in part upon my presentation at the Centennial Celebration delivered at Suffolk University Law School's Conference on the Globalization of Legal Education on January 25, 2007 as well as an article I wrote with Thomas Koenig for a Syracuse Law Review Symposium on Lawyer Unhappiness. I would like to thank Stephen Hicks, my colleague and former teacher for organizing the conference on *Globalization and the U.S. Law School: Comparative and Cultural Perspectives, 1906–2006*. I would like to thank Thomas H. Koenig of Northeastern who help me compile the data reported in this article. I would like to thank my colleagues Stephen Hicks, Miquel Shor, and Jeffrey Lipshaw for their critical comments. Thanks also to Gail and Howard Straw for their encouragement and support. This chapter draws upon themes in work I have done with Thomas H. Koenig of Northeastern University. I also appreciate the assistance of Beth Bowers, University Archivist as well as Julia Collins Associate University Archivist of the Moakley Library and Suffolk University Archives. Shannon Downey, John Hebb, Meaghan Marfioni, Nicole Chiesa provided expert research and editorial assistance. Nicole Chiesa provided research as well as editorial assistance through several different stages of this piece. I would also like to thank Professor Stephen Hicks and Attorney Steven Cohen for their suggestions. Chryss J. Knowles also provided invaluable editorial assistance.

[3] William Blake, *Auguries of Innocence*, (1803) last visited Sept. 20, 2007) http://www.artofeurope.com/blake/bla3.htm.

[4] ALFRED Z. REED, PRESENT-DAY LAW SCHOOLS IN THE UNITED STATES AND CANADA 198 (1928).

open American legal education schools to a more diversified student population. In no other city did the conflict over equality of educational opportunity generate as much heat and national attention as Suffolk's war with Harvard and its allies during the 1920s.

Across the Charles River from Harvard University Law School, Suffolk Law School opened in its doors in 1906. This chapter examines the untold story of Suffolk University Law School's counter hegemonic method of legal education. This is the story of how Gleason Archer and his allies in the night law school movement challenged the hegemony of patrician legal education by opening the legal profession to lower and working class students from many different ethnic groups. Archer's crusade to open law schools helped to transform the legal profession from a system of sponsored mobility based upon class to a more diversified field where achievement played a more important role. The story of Suffolk's meteoric rise from an evening law school located in a tenement to a world class institution in the hub of Boston's legal world is one of the greatest stories never told in the history of legal education.

I. Harvard and the Elite Law Schools as Patrician Elites

Law schools were not the dominant method of educating lawyers throughout much of this country's history. Professional law schools were unknown until 1748 when Judge Reeve founded the Litchfield Law School in Litchfield, Connecticut, which graduated "more than 1,000 lawyers before it closed its doors in 1833."[5] Litchfield claimed as alumni Aaron Burr, three U.S. Supreme Court Justices, one hundred one members of the U.S. House of Representatives, twenty-eight U.S. Senators, six Cabinet members, and thirteen chief justices of state supreme courts.[6] Litchfield was the training ground for young white men who were "gentlemen distinguished no less as Statesmen than Civilians."[7]

The first American university-affiliated law schools were the College of William and Mary, founded in 1779; followed by The University of Pennsylvania Law School, founded in 1790 and Harvard University's law school,

5 David D. Garner, *The Continuing Vitality of the Case Method in the Twenty-First Century*, 2000 BYU EDUC. & L. J. 307, 313 (2000).

6 Id.

7 LITCHFIELD HISTORICAL SOCIETY, A HISTORY OF THE LITCHFIELD LAW SCHOOL (last visited Feb. 20, 2006), http://www.litchfieldhistoricalsociety.org/history/histlawschool.html.

established in 1817.[8] As late as 1860, only 1,200 students attended America's law schools.[9] During the late nineteenth century, the number of law students doubled as a result of industrialization. [10] Industrialization provided attorneys with the opportunity to counsel large corporations and mediate relations with government regulators.[11]

By the late nineteenth century, the number of law schools grew steadily, but most lawyers came to the law through law office apprenticeships.[12] By 1870, there were 31 U.S. law schools and 51 by 1880.[13] Most of the early law schools "were proprietary, taught by persons who were full-time practitioners or judges." [14]

Formal legal training was needed after the Civil War as America underwent a "fundamental transformation" from a relatively static agrarian society to a dynamic, developing economy.[15] By the early twentieth century, the blueblood dynasties, and large corporations were beginning to turn to lawyers who were trained at "Class 'A' Law Schools" such as Harvard."[16] New technologies, the growth of giant corporations, large-scale immigration, and the expansion of the role of government created complicated struggles that were frequently mediated by attorneys. The old apprenticeship system could not supply enough sophisticated lawyers to apply the increasingly complex legal concepts that were being created.

Most lawyers at the beginning of the nineteenth century were college-bred men chosen through a system of sponsored mobility. The established elite recommended them to the bar based on certain criteria such as family lineage or school ties. An astounding ninety percent of the lawyers admitted to practice in Boston from 1780 to 1817 were Harvard College men.[17] "It should be the aim of the University's Law School," Harvard President Charles Eliot declared in 1875, "to train young men of good preliminary education and average ability, taken by the hundred, for the higher walks of the profession."[18]

---

[8] HARVARD UNIVERSITY, HISTORY OF HARVARD UNIVERSITY LAW SCHOOL (last visited April 6, 2006) http://en.wikipedia.org/wiki/Harvard_Law_School#History.

[9] Id. at 198.

[10] ALFRED Z. REED, PRESIDENT-DAY LAW SCHOOLS IN THE UNITED STATES AND CANADA 198 (1928).

[11] Robert Stevens, *Law Schools and Legal Education, 1879–1979: Lectures in Honor of 100 Years of Valparaiso Law School,* 14 VAL. U.L. REV. 179 (1979–1980).

[12] Erwin N. Griswold, *Legal Education: 1878–1978,* 64 A.B.A.J. 1051, 1051 (1978).

[13] Id.

[14] Id.

[15] MORTON HORWITZ, THE TRANSFORMATION OF AMERICAN LAW: 1780–1860 (1976).

[16] Arthur L. Corbin, *Democracy and Education for the Bar,* 4 AM L. SCH. REV. 725, 726 (1915–1922).

[17] Id. at 194–5.

[18] Anthony Chase, *The Birth of the Modern Law School,* 23 AM. J. LEGAL HIST. 336, 337 (1979).

Harvard's Case Law System

Christopher Columbus Langdell, later to become Dean of Harvard Law School, developed the case law system that swept the nation. While Harvard classes employed questions and answers designed to teach the student to "think like a lawyer," Suffolk students were not permitted to ask more than two questions per night of their lecturers. Harvard University Law School soon became the Vatican City or Holy See of the law school world with its invention of the case method for college educated men. Langdell, a New York City practitioner who was appointed to the Harvard law faculty in 1870, apparently invented the case method of instruction[19] in the first contracts class he taught at Harvard:

> "Mr. Fox, will you state the facts in the case of *Payne v. Cave?"* That simple question marked the beginning of a revolution in legal education. In 1870, Professor Christopher Columbus Langdell, in the first contracts class he taught at Harvard Law School, put the question to a student and forever changed the way lawyers learned their craft. No longer would law students sit passively and take notes while their professor lectured or read out of a legal treatise. Langdell's students read the reports of actual court cases and were required to discuss them in class.[20]

Christopher Columbus Langdell became, in effect, the Pope of American Legal Education and his students became Papal Legates exporting the case method as professors in law schools around the country. With the assistance of Langdell's student disciples, men like "John H. Wigmore took the case method to Northwestern; Eugene Wambaugh to the State University of Iowa ... and Kenner [who] stormed the citadel at Columbia."[21]

---

[19] Christopher Columbus Langdell "entered Harvard in 1848, but left in 1849 to become a teacher, and was afterward graduated at the law school in 1853. He then practiced in New York City till 1870, when he became professor of jurisprudence, and dean of the law faculty, at Harvard. He was given his degree of A. B., as a member of the class of 1851, in 1870, and that of LL.D. in 1875. Professor Langdell published SELECTION OF CASES ON THE LAW OF CONTRACTS (2 parts, Boston, 1870; enlarged ed., 1877); CASES ON SALES (1872); SUMMARY OF EQUITY PLEADING (Cambridge, 1877; 2d ed., 1883); and CASES IN EQUITY PLEADING (printed privately, 1878)." Appleton's Encyclopedia, *Christopher Columbus Langdell* (last visited Oct. 19, 2007) http://famousamericans.netchristophercolumbuslangdell/.

[20] Christopher Columbus Langdell, 6 AMERICAN LAW ENCYCLOPEDIA ONLINE, http://law.jrank.org/pages/8072/Langdell-Christopher-Columbus.html (last visited Oct. 19, 2007).

[21] LAWRENCE M. FRIEDMAN, A HISTORY OF AMERICAN LAW 470–71 (3d ed. 2005).

University-educated law students studied appellate cases from textbooks that featured few references to public law or social policy.[22] The Harvard case law method eschewed discussions of social justice in favor of "rules, principles, and cases laid out in abstract, orderly systems."[23] Langdell compiled a collection of appellate opinions into the first casebook published devoid of textual notes, explanations, or even basic summaries of doctrine.[24] The case law system was part of a wider social movement to revitalize the law for a rapidly industrializing America:[25]

> Christopher Columbus Langdell became the dean of Harvard Law School, and began to restructure legal scholarship and the teaching of law … The consolidation battles of the railroads, waged by legal battalions on both sides, continued to scandalize the New York bar. The Association of the Bar of the City of New York (the City Bar) was founded in response to revelations of widespread political and judicial corruption in the city. Finally, states were beginning to institute the first written bar exams. The very conception of the law was changing, and reform was in the air.[26]

Harvard was the first law school to reconceptualize legal education as a science and law students as budding scientists. Law school students uncovered general principles of law from a close study of cases rather than learn practical pleading and principles as apprentices under the supervision of seasoned members of the practicing bar:

> The question at issue for over twenty years now is what Langdell might have meant when he said that 'law, considered as a science, consists of certain principles or doctrines,' that 'all the available materials' of legal science 'are contained in printed books,' and that 'the library is ... to

---

[22] Robert Stevens, Law School: Legal Education in America from the 1850s to the 1980s 61 (1983) (describing the case law system of legal education).
[23] Jean Stefancic & Richard Delgado, How Lawyers Lose Their Way 33 (2005).
[24] Christopher Columbus Langdell, A Selection of Cases on the Law of Contracts (1871) (available at http://books.google.com/books?id=0RdmOi8BQB0C&pg=PR1&dq=Langdell+Contracts+Cases&sig=4QeeD0jdTMBtgDfo4wQC2GnKodc (Google book search).
[25] Lawrence M. Friedman, A History of American Law 570–571 (3d ed. 2005) (noting all the case law system of legal education displaced the older apprenticeship system). *See also* Gerald P. Moran, *A Radical Theory of Jurisprudence: The 'Decision maker' as the Source of Law—The Ohio Supreme court's Adoption of the Spendthrift Trust Doctrine as a Model,* 30 Akron L. Rev. 349, 410 (1997) (describing Langdell's "scientifically" oriented case method at Harvard Law School).
[26] Laura I Appleman, *German Scholarship and Legal Reform Shaped Our System of Legal Education,* 39 N. Engl. L. Rev. 251, 251 (2005).

> us all that the laboratories of the university are to the chemists and physicists, all that the museum of natural history is to the zoologists, all that the botanical garden is to the botanists.' To the post-Realist academic lawyer, Langdell's use of 'science' seems to be a reference to scientific empiricism. Thus, the man seems to be confused, for the laboratory of an empirically based science of law would need to be focused, not in the library, but in the courts, legislatures, agencies, and law offices where the law in action is made. In such a world, a thoroughgoing empiricism would treat the cases that expound appellate court doctrine as the irreducible facts because of which that doctrine, the explanatory apparatus of case law theory, would be tested for truth.[27]

The case law system was based upon the assumption that there were core principles which could be uncovered through systematic analysis that removed emotional considerations, larger societal debates and personal conceptions of right and wrong from legal thought. Harvard's case law system revolutionized legal education and combined with other innovations such as "pre-legal educational requirements, entrance and exit exams, a phased curriculum, full-time faculty, and a lengthened course of study" to upgrade legal education during the period from 1870 to 1920.[28] Harvard was the trend setter in elite legal education during the formative era of Suffolk evening law school.

II. Suffolk's Counter-Hegemonic Challenge to the Patrician Legal Elite

Archer castigated Harvard's case law system as a fashion that started at Harvard but "was shortly adopted by all law schools that delight to borrow the plumage of the great."[29] Archer crowed that his Suffolk evening law school had grown to be the "largest law school in the world" through a completely different method of teaching law, the Suffolk Method.[30] Suffolk Law School, founded in 1906, described itself as "opportunity's open door" for males who had to work for a living, lacked educational credentials, or who could not afford the higher tuition of the day schools. Suffolk was formed during the Progressive Era, which was the "Golden Age for law school establishment" as the number

---

[27] John Henry Schlegel, *Langdell's Audo-da-fe,* 17 LAW & HIST. REV. 1 (1999) (last Visited Sept. 28, 2007), http://www.historycooperative.org/journals/lhr/17.1/schlegel.html.

[28] Laura I Appleman, *German Scholarship and Legal Reform Shaped Our System of Legal Education,* 39 N. ENGL. L. REV. 251, 253 (2005).

[29] Id. at 1.

[30] Id.

of law schools more than doubled from 61 in 1890 to 124 by 1910.[31] Much of this growth was due to the rise of night law schools. Suffolk evening law school was an attractive option for those aspiring to state government service because of its location next to Massachusetts' Statehouse. Thomas J. Boynton, formerly U.S. Attorney for Massachusetts and later the Attorney General of Massachusetts, was selected by Dean Gleason Archer to become a member of the school's Board of Trustees.[32] Boynton used populist themes of equality in his fund raising appeal to potential Suffolk donors:

> Did you ever stop to think that the ignorant leader is a grave menace to this and to every other community? Did you ever think that to endow schools for the favored few and utterly to neglect the multitude is to prevent the masses from having sound leaders, therefore, delivering them over to designing agitators?[33]

The Evening Law School Movement

Evening law schools opened in nearly every major American city in the late nineteenth century and early decades of the twentieth century to accommodate the aspirations of men who could only attend classes at night. Between 1901 and 1906, when Suffolk Evening Law School was in its infancy, Brooklyn Law School (1901), Fordham (1906) and the evening division of the New York Law School (1904) were also founded. All of these law schools were founded within a few decades of Harvard University Law School's development of the modern law school.[34]

Gleason Archer opened Archer's Evening Law School in Roxbury only a few months after graduating from Boston University Law School. [35] He opened the

---

[31] Dorothy E. Finnegan, *Raising and Leveling the Bar: Standards, Access, and the YMCA Evening Law Schools, 1890–1940*, 55 J. LEGAL EDUC. 208, 208 (2005).

[32] GLEASON L. ARCHER, SUFFOLK LAW ALUMNI DIRECTORY AND FIVE-YEAR BOOK, NO. 1 (1906–1928) (published by Suffolk Law Alumni Association, Boston, Massachusetts, 1928) at 23 (on file with the authors).

[33] Thomas Koenig & Michael Rustad, *The Challenge to Hierarchy in Legal Education: Suffolk and the Night Law School Movement*, 7 RESEARCH IN LAW, DEVIANCE, AND SOCIAL CONTROL 189, 206 (1985) (quoting Massachusetts Attorney General Thomas Boynton).

[34] *See generally*, Anthony Chase, *The Birth of the Modern Law School*, 23 AM. J. LEGAL HIST. 336, 337 (1979).

[35] David Robbins writes about the opening night: "That warm night as the lecture closed, all nine auditors were glued to their seats—by the new varnish on Archer's second-hand chairs. Once they tore themselves away [from their studied] however, word spread that there was something more than varnish holding men to their places in the young educator's front room." DAVID L. ROBBINS, A HISTORY OF SUFFOLK UNIVERSITY (1906–2006) 23 (2006).

Archer Evening Law School on September 19, 1906 enrolling nine students who attended classes in Archer's apartment at 6 Alpine Street in Roxbury, a neighborhood of Boston, Massachusetts. Roxbury was one of the oldest towns founded in the Massachusetts Bay Colony in 1630.

Suffolk's Modest Beginnings

Gleason Archer taught his law school classes in his living room and his only means of advertisement was a sign displayed in the bay window of his apartment building and simple newspaper notices.[36] Robert Healey, a child of Irish immigrants born in 1883, was one of Archer's first students enrolling in 1907. Healey worked by day as a machinist in an iron foundry, enrolled in Gleason Archer's Evening Law School in 1907 and graduated in 1910.[37] By 1918, Healey opened his own law office at 6 Beacon Street.[38] Thaddeus Alexander Kitchener, an immigrant from Kingston Jamaica and a janitor at Simmons College was a member of the Class of 1913.[39] Ole Dahl, a Norwegian immigrant, who painted houses by day, was one of Archer's first students and supposedly asked Archer: "Can you learn me anything?"[40] Dahl graduated in 1910 with Suffolk's second graduating class:

> Ole Martin Dahl was born between 1869 and 1875 in Norway, coming to the United States in 1890. In 1905, he answered an advertisement for a law class to be taught by Gleason Archer. By this time, he was working as a house painter and decorator, and Gleason Archer visited him at his shop in response to his inquiry about the law class. Archer writes that Ole Dahl 'had ruddy cheeks and a good natured face, altogether prepossessing except that his English was very faulty,' and that Ole was concerned that he was too old (at least 30 years old) to be taught about law. Despite these concerns, Ole Dahl attended Archer's

---

[36] Id.

[37] This account is based upon records in the Suffolk University archives compiled by Beth Bowers, Suffolk University Law School Archivist. See, Beth Bowers, *Robert Timothy Healey, Suffolk Law School (1910)* (unpublished manuscript 2006) (on file with the authors).

[38] Id.

[39] Beth Bowers, Suffolk University Law School Archives, Profile *of Thaddeus Alexander Kitchener, Class of 1913* (on file with the authors).

[40] JOSEPH F. KETT, THE PURSUIT OF KNOWLEDGE UNDER DIFFICULTIES: FROM SELF-IMPROVEMENT TO ADULT EDUCATION IN AMERICA 1750–1990 267 (1994) (describing Archer's early tribulations in starting Suffolk Law School).

first law class in October of 1905, and enrolled at Suffolk Law School at its inception in September of 1906.[41]

Roxbury was then a Boston neighborhood composed largely of working class immigrants but by the early twentieth century was the home of a growing Jewish population.[42] Archer's open admission policy was out of necessity because he had "to settle for the most disadvantaged students."[43] Grammar school graduates studied alongside the college educated in a Social Darwinist system of contest mobility. Suffolk Law School's Class of 1912, for example, consisted of eight grammar school graduates, four high school graduates and only two students with some college education.[44] Archer's law school, which charged only $45 a year, was "among the cheapest in the nation."[45] Two years after Archer began his evening law school; his law partner Arthur Winfield joined him on the "faculty" in the spring of 1907.[46] In 1907, Archer renamed his business enterprise "Suffolk Evening Law School" and reopened the school in its new home at 53 Tremont Street on September 30, 1907.[47]

Archer practiced law by day and his offices served double duty as classrooms three nights a week.[48] In March of 1909, Archer again moved his law school, this time to The Tremont Temple Baptist Church,[49] only a block from the current home of Suffolk University Law School's $70 million building. Archer first took the microphone as a substitute speaker at [Boston's] WBZ-WBZA in 1929, but was soon a regular orator who hobnobbed with media stars.[50] Archer was a man of unusual energy and talents:

---

41 Ole Martin Dahl, Suffolk Law School 1910, Suffolk University Archives, Early Student Research Project (1906) (on filed with the authors).

42 Wikipedia, Roxbury, Massachusetts http://en.wikipedia.org/wiki/Roxbury,_Massachusetts (last visited Oct. 20, 2007).

43 Kett, *The Pursuit of Knowledge*, Id. at 267.

44 Beth Bower University Archivist, *Research on Early Suffolk Law School Graduates* (Oct. 13, 2006) (unpublished report on file with the authors).

45 Id.

46 David L. Robbins, a history of suffolk University (1906–2006) 24 (2006).

47 Gleason L. Archer, Suffolk Law Alumni Directory and Five-Year Book, No. 1 (1906–1928) at 16 (published by Suffolk Law Alumni Association, Boston, Massachusetts, 1928) at 13 (recounting Dean Archer's chronology of the history of Suffolk Law School first two decades) (on file with the authors).

48 David L. Robbins, a history of suffolk University (1906–2006) 24 (2006) (describing the growth of Suffolk Evening Law School and its move to Tremont Street).

49 Gleason Archer, Building a School, Id. at 12.

> The new location, combined with Archer's genius for obtaining fee publicity, provided
> – a fillip to attendance. The Dean, as he soon styled himself, was indefatigable. He taught and handled all administrative duties. He courted political speakers, baited suffragettes,
> – raced trains in his car, and gave away scholarships by popular vote—anything to call
> – attention to his school.[51]

Archer raised funds for Suffolk Law School on his NBC Radio program where he implored his listeners to give "poor boys a chance." Archer, who wrote the leading book on the history of radio, used the radio and the print media for recruitment and fund-raising.

Suffolk Becomes the Largest Law School in the World

By the 1920s, Suffolk evening law school had grown to be the largest law school in the world. Dean Gleason Archer erected a large neon sign proclaiming the location of Suffolk Law School. To raise funds for his fledging law school, Archer converted the law school auditorium into the "Suffolk Theatre." He showed first-run motion pictures to the public in the school's auditorium during off-hours when classes were not in session.[52] Archer placed advertisements for "Boston's new picture house" which showed many productions "of the film stars in their big productions."[53] Archer not only issued individual tickets of admission to his law school classes each semester, but he also sold day of performance tickets for movies shown in the law school auditorium.

Archer imported the largest pipe organ in New England in 1921 for the sum of $50,000 and advertised that it would produce the "finest music ever heard in any Boston picture house."[54] The Suffolk Movie Theatre, which Archer dubbed "Boston's Ideal Picture House featured the then screen idol Earle Williams in *Diamonds Adrift*."[55] By the mid-1920's, Gleason Archer was not

---

50 DAVID L. ROBBINS, A HISTORY OF SUFFOLK UNIVERSITY (1906–2006) 30 (2006) (describing Archer's pioneering talks on law topics on radio and particularly "his hard-line broadcasts on crime and criminal law" which made him a sensation).

51 Id. at 25.

52 *Suffolk Theatre*, BOSTON GLOBE (April 17, 1921) (on file with the authors).

53 Id.

54 *Suffolk Theatre*, Cambridge Tribune, (July 18, 1921) (on file with the authors).

55 *Advertisement for Suffolk Theatre*, BOSTON GLOBE (April 17, 1921) (on file with the authors).

only the Dean of the largest U.S. law school, but also President of the National Association of Day and Evening Law Schools (NADEL),[56] an organization that was established "to counterbalance the AALS" and to oppose its efforts to exclude the sons of the working class in the name of educational quality.[57]

Archer was a public relations genius who prefigured today's television evangelists in his charisma and his ability to raise money. He urged his listeners on the NBC network to send him contributions so he could create scholarships to give poor boys a chance. Archer's steady stream of books and speeches, planted news stories, and the construction of a neon sign on the roof so large it could be seen from Harvard's classrooms in Cambridge irritated members of the elite bar. In 1937, he enrolled crooner Rudy Vallee, the host of the world's most popular radio talk show, [58] as a publicity stunt.[59]

Archer's greatest public relations ploy was his blatant manipulation of the Boston press by staging a public debate at the Tremont Temple on the desirability of admitting women to law school. Archer took the negative position and won the debate handily. Infuriated women's rights advocates demanded the right to attend law school attacking Archer in the Boston newspapers.[60] Archer gloated privately "[n]othing could have been more timely or valuable as publicity for the school."[61] Behind the scenes, Archer was secretly taking advantage of the controversy he had stirred up by helping his law partner Arthur W. McLean found Portia, a for profit evening law school for women.[62] Portia, like Suffolk, became an overnight success. Portia educated more American women attorneys than any other U.S. law school throughout the 1920s and 1930s.[63] By the close of the 1920s, one in three women lawyers in America had been educated at Portia Evening Law School.[64]

---

56 David L. Robbins, A history of suffolk University (1906–2006) 30 (2006).

57 Id.

58 "The Fleischmann Hour," nationally known as the Rudy Vallee Hour—the first-ever radio talk show—debuted in 1928 and gained 200 million listeners. It was a live variety revue and Rudy's guests were a mixture of the famous and the unknown. He was the first to invite black musicians to be on his show, and in appreciation, artists such as Louis Armstrong and Josephine Baker invited Rudy to their clubs in Harlem." Rudy Vallee Biography (last visited Oct. 3, 2007), http://www.rudyvallee.com/bio.html.

59 Suffolk Centennial Timeline (last visited Oct. 3, 2007), http://www.law.suffolk.edu/about/history/image.cfm?PhotoNum=SU-0158.

60 Id. at 630.

61 Gleason Archer, Building a School: A fearless portrayal of men and events in the old bay state 82, 83 (1919).

62 Id.

63 Ronald Chester, *Women Lawyers in the Urban Bar: An Oral History*, 18 New Engl L. Rev. 521, 527 (1982–83)

64 Id.

While Harvard University Law School required its patrician students to be college graduates, Archer specialized in giving the poor boy a chance. Archer's evening law school was equal opportunity's open door for unskilled workers, factory workers, artisans, clerks, and worthy male entrants from a wide variety of immigrant groups. Under Suffolk's open admissions policy, any student who desired to study law—and could afford the tuition—was allowed to compete in a tournament where twenty percent or fewer graduated.

While the evening schools catered to the relative disadvantaged members of the lower middle class and working class, Harvard Law School was for wealthy elites. Harvard required that its gentlemen law students earn a bachelor's degree before admission. Harvard's administration wanted a school that would foster the development of a "responsible social elite." Felix Frankfurter, a Professor at the Law School and later a U.S. Supreme Court stated that if you wanted top-line groceries you shopped at "Magruder's ... if you wanted to get a lot of first class lawyers, you went to Harvard Law School."[65] In its early years, Suffolk was too insignificant to be noticed by Harvard's overseers.

The "Suffolk Method" of Teaching Black Letter Law

In 1924, Archer wrote a bulletin entitled, the "Suffolk Law School System vs. Case System of Teaching Law."[66] The case method, in Archer's opinion, was designed for "college graduates only who were expected to devote all their time, both day and evening, for three years to the study of law."[67] He castigated the case system for requiring students to study overly "technical, bewildering" cases often "of great length."[68]

Archer was not alone in criticizing the case law system. The legal realist jurist Jerome Frank argued "American legal education went badly wrong when it was seduced by a brilliant neurotic [Christopher Columbus Langdell]."[69] While cases were valuable to read, they were not an efficient means of teaching law. The case law approach was a mental "pick and shovel" method that resulted in a "pitiful waste of effort," in Archer's view:[70]

---

[65] FELIX FRANKFURTER, FELIX FRANKFURTER REMINISCES, 248–49 (Harlan Phillips ed., 1960).

[66] Gleason L. Archer, LL.B, Dean and Founder, SUFFOLK LAW SCHOOL SYSTEM VS. CASE SYSTEM OF TEACHING LAW (Oct. 31, 1924) (unpublished document found in Suffolk Law School archives).

[67] Id.

[68] Id.

[69] Thomas J. O'Toole, *Realistic Legal Education* 54 A.B.A. J. 774, 774 (1968) (quoting Jerome Frank as maintaining that "something of immense worth was lost when our leading law schools wholly abandoned the legal apprenticeship system") (available on Hein online).

[70] Gleason L. Archer, Suffolk Law System, Id.

> In other lines of educational training, we believe in taking advantage of the accumulated wisdom of past generations. To do otherwise would be a waste of precious time and energy. The great a waste is involved in the case method may be illustrated thus: A student spends his day and evening in earnest study of cases assigned, and at the end of that time has not gleaned as much law as a professor could give him in five minutes.[71]

The case law system, Archer argued, caused the student to remember, "That is something like the case of *Jones v. Brown* or perhaps like *Smith v. Green*."[72] The Harvard student might remember the cases but forget the underlying principles so that reliance on reading cases was "much inferior" to teaching students a black letter knowledge of the principles of law.[73]

Archer's War with Harvard's Crimson Octopus

Archer's evening law school teetered at the brink of insolvency in 1912 because the Massachusetts Bar Examiners refused to grade the examination of Suffolk graduates. Archer applied to the Massachusetts State Legislature for the power to grant degrees in January of 1912. [74] Suffolk's charter bill passed the Massachusetts House of Representatives on February 13, 1912 and a week later was approved by the Senate.[75] In March of 1912, the Suffolk bill was vetoed by Governor Eugene Foss.[76] During the first week of January in 1912, Archer reorganized his law school business as a corporation, a move necessary to improve Suffolk's chance of earning degree-conferring powers from the state legislature.[77] Twenty-three out of twenty-five Massachusetts state representatives who voted against the Suffolk Bill were college graduates. [78] Even though

---

71 JOSEPH TINNELLY, PART-TIME EDUCATION: A STUDY OF THE PROBLEM OF EVENING LAW STUDENTS 13 (1957).

72 Id.

73 Id.

74 GLEASON L. ARCHER, THE EDUCATIONAL OCTOPUS: A FEARLESS PORTRAYAL OF MEN & EVENTS IN THE OLD BAY STATE 1906–1915 (1915).

75 Id.

76 Eugene N. Foss, who married the daughter of a prominent industrialist, became President of Sturtevant "America's first fan company." Sturtevant, http://www.sturtevantfan.com/foss.html (last visited Oct. 20, 2007). Foss, who was originally a Republican was elected Massachusetts Governor in 1911. Shortly after Foss vetoed the Suffolk Bill, he dispatched twelve companies of the Massachusetts Militia to quell labor unrest during the 1912 Lawrence mill strike; Governor Foss dispatched twelve companies of the Massachusetts Militia. Id.

77 GLEASON L. ARCHER, THE EDUCATIONAL OCTOPUS, Id.

78 Id. at 186.

the Suffolk Bill passed, Governor Eugene Foss vetoed it and Archer reapplied for accreditation the next year.[79]

Archer used vivid populist images in explaining Harvard's role in blocking his students' aspirations. Harvard's President Lawrence Lowell testified against the Suffolk degree bill, which Archer characterized as the work of the mighty "educational octopus set out to crush the fledgling educational institution."[80] Harvard was guarding the "sacred rights of the privileged class that must be protected against the assaults of the boorish common people."[81] In Gleason Archer's autobiography, written at age 35, he described his struggles against Harvard's crimson octopus to gain accreditation in Massachusetts:

> Gleason Archer … saw two main dangers in society: the 'reds' (Communists) and the 'crimsons' (Harvard). "Opening law schools to the poor was his … bulwark against the encroachment of both of these sinister forces.[82]

Archer denounced Harvard as a "spoiled child" of the state legislature that was the beneficiary of millions of dollars of tax rebates.[83] Harvard's "crimson tentacles" extended "from Committee Room to Committee Room, reaching from the halls of legislation to the Governor's Office."[84] Harvard's steadfast opposition to Suffolk was partly because of the threat this fledgling institution posed to Boston's YMCA Law School. The YMCA Law School was a "respectable" evening school that catered to worthy Protestant males. The YMCA. Law School (later to become Northeastern University) drew college men who lacked the resources to attend Harvard University Law School or Boston University Law School. Dean Ames of Harvard and Dean Bennett of Boston University served on the school's advisory board.[85]

Harvard's sponsorship of the YMCA Law School was based upon Boston Brahmin lawyers' sense of *noblese obliges*. Elihu Root, Harvard Law professor and statesman, reasoned that the stability of American institutions "depended upon leaving the road open, however difficult it may be, for men of genuine ability to satisfy their ambitions either in the profession of law or in public

---

79 Id.
80 Id. at 277.
81 Id.
82 ROBERT STEVENS, LAW SCHOOL 80 (1983).
83 Id.
84 Id.
85 ROBERT STEVENS, LAW SCHOOL: LEGAL EDUCATION IN AMERICA FROM THE 1850'S TO THE 1980'S 80–81 (1983).

service."[86] The 1917 YMCA class drew college educated students from "100 towns and cities of New England, the Southern and Western states and foreign countries,"[87] while Archer's grammar school educated students were largely local Bostonians. In contrast to Suffolk, the YMCA Law School had no problem receiving degree-granting powers in 1904 because its distinguished faculty was composed entirely of Harvard and Boston University graduates.[88] Louis Brandeis, a Harvard Law School professor and later a U.S. Supreme Court Justice, lectured to the Protestant boys attending the YMCA Law School as did Robert Gray Dodge, the founding name partner of one of Boston's venerable law firm, Ropes and Gray.[89]

Many YMCA graduates had preliminary educations from such reputable institutions as Brown, Massachusetts Institute of Technology (MIT), and Amherst College, in contrast to most evening students who were fortunate to hold a high school degree. By 1903, the Boston YMCA Evening Law School had "enrolled more than 662 men, graduated 32, and earned the right to confer degrees from the state legislature." [90] The goal of the school was to "give every ambitious man who is willing to sacrifice for the achievement of an educational ideal … at a price he can afford to pay." [91]

The Massachusetts Legislature passed the Suffolk Bill in 1913, which newly elected Governor David Walsh, signed.[92] Suffolk's degree granting powers allowed it not only to survive, but also to flourish. In 1914, only a year after it received its charter, the school purchased its own building at 45 Mount Vernon Street.[93] In 1919, Archer purchased a building site at the corner of Temple and Derne Street on Boston's Beacon Hill.[94] Governor Calvin Coolidge, who had just been named as the Vice Presidential candidate on the Republican ticket, laid the corner stone for Suffolk's new building on August 4, 1920.[95] Archer was a shrewd politician who appointed Joseph Francis

---

86 Arthur L. Corbin, *Democracy and Education for the Bar* 4 Am. L. School Rev. 725, 733 (1921)
87 Id.
88 Michael Rustad & Thomas Koenig, *The Impact of History on Contemporary Prestige Images of Boston's Law Schools*, Id. at 628.
89 Id. at 628.
90 Dorothy E. Finnegan, *Raising and Leveling the Bar: Standards, Access, and the YMCA Evening Law Schools, 1890–1940*, 55 J. Legal Educ. 208, 216 (2005).
91 Id. at 218.
92 Id.
93 Id.
94 Gleason L. Archer, Suffolk Law Alumni Directory and Five-Year Book No. 1, 1906–1928 (Suffolk Law Alumni Association, Boston, Massachusetts) at 14 (on file with the authors).
95 Id.

O'Connell to the faculty and later to Suffolk Law School's Board of Trustees. O'Connell, an 1896 graduate of Harvard Law School, was elected to the U.S. Congress as a representative from Massachusetts in 1907–11. O'Connell was a strong advocate for Suffolk and became Vice President of its Board of Trustees in the early 1920s. Suffolk's new building was crowded with an influx of veterans from World War I and other workers from a wide variety of occupations.[96]

Suffolk Law School's Battle with the AALS & ABA

Suffolk was to face an even greater challenged in the national arena pitted against the American Bar Association (ABA). At its first organizing meeting in 1878, the ABA recommended higher standards in legal education. The ABA's Section on Legal Section sought to upgrade legal education by requiring students to have graduated from high school and complete a minimum of three years of law school.[97] At their 1919 Annual Meeting, held at Boston's Public Library, the section discussed "The Best Way to Secure a Broad, Liberal Education for American Lawyer."[98] J.C. Collins, an ABA delegate from Rhode Island, expressed concerns about the increasing numbers of new immigrants entering the bar:

> We had a Bar examination two years ago, in which we happened to have a small number of Candidates, and among them there were two of French-Canadian extraction; two of Italian extraction; one of Portuguese extraction; one of Roumanian (sic) extraction; and I believe one Lithuanian; one of pure American extraction, and two whose parents came from the British Empire...Now the same standard of education, preparatory, which might fit the young man born of American ancestry, would not, in my opinion, be equally good for the young man who came from Central Europe....The result is that we have about 40 per cent of the candidates, generally, who do not pass the examination.[99]

Suffolk enrolled American Indians, African-Americans and Asian-Americans,

---

96 DAVID L. ROBBINS, A HISTORY OF SUFFOLK UNIVERSITY (1906–2006) 24 (2006)

97 ROBERT STEVENS, LAW SCHOOL: LEGAL EDUCATION IN AMERICA FROM THE 1850S TO THE 1980S 96 (1983).

98 *Proceedings of the Section of Legal Education,* 6 A.B.A.J. 64 (1920).

99 Id. at 65–67.

as well as poor Catholics and Jews. Racism and open animosity toward ethnic lawyers increased the vehemence of the attacks on the evening schools:

> The influx of Catholics, Jews, and other newly arrived aliens from Southern and Eastern Europe was a tremendous threat for American WASPs. Unlike immigrants from similarly Anglo-Saxon countries (England, Scotland, Norway, etc.), these unfamiliar immigrants were categorized as "other" and "foreign" in a way that previous arrivals were not ... Anti-alien sentiments were strong in the cities, where the elites saw the new arrivals as 'dispirited breeders of poverty, crime, and political corruption, and simultaneously as peculiarly powerful subversives whose foreign ideologies were undermining American society.' ... These fears rang loud in the mind of law's elite, who saw themselves as representatives of the people, protecting against unlawful behavior. The legal elite felt that they had the role of cultural caretakers, as a guardian needed to preserve Anglo-American norms and mores.[100]

The ABA Section of Legal Education delegated many of its functions to the Association of American Law Schools (AALS), which was founded in 1900[101] in order to upgrade the educational standards of law schools. In 1900, a coalition of thirty-two University-based institutions of legal education founded the American Association of Law Schools (AALS).[102] Harvard Law School's James Bradley Thayer was elected as first President of the AALS. The ABA and the AALS used the ideology of raising educational standards rather than a frontal attack on new immigrants and the unworthy poor seeking admission to the bar. The theme chosen for the 1932 meetings of the Section on Legal Education of the American Bar Association was "Overcrowding of the Bar and What Should Be Done About It?"[103] The ABA Legal Section's proceedings demonstrated beyond a reasonable doubt that the ABA's goal was to eliminate night schools.

As a result, Archer, in his usual defiant fashion, enrolled new immigrants, blacks, American Indians, Jews, and Asian-Americans, as well as poor Catholics and new immigrants from every race and creed. Evening law schools

---

[100] Laura I Appleman, *German Scholarship and Legal Reform Shaped Our System of Legal Education*, 39 N. ENGL. L. REV. 251, 266 (2005).

[101] American Association of Law Schools, *What is the AALS?* (last visited April 2, 2006), http://www.aals.org/about.php.

[102] Id.

[103] Young B. Smith and James Grafton Rogers, *The Overcrowding of the Bar and What Can Be Done About It.*, 7 ABA REPORTS 565 (1932).

were the avenue of upward mobility for many ambitious African-American students. Prominent Arkansas African-American lawyers George Napier Perkins and Alexander L. Burnett attended evening law schools.[104] The backlash against these groups entering a previously all Anglo-Saxon sphere was immediate. Big firms excluded these new entrants and, as a result, many new evening law schools practiced as solo practitioners. Jewish and Catholic new immigrant lawyers of lower-class origin were concentrated among the urban solo practitioners whose behavior was unethical. Suffolk graduates were frequently accused of having low ethical standards.

The patrician bar's campaign against evening law school graduates was sometimes openly racist and decidedly anti-Semitic. A few lions of the bar warned of the increase in Jewish lawyers in New York City and their flooding of the organized bar. The elite bar's true concern was racism. The AALS framed the issue as quality of legal education, rather than excluding the "unworthy" ethnic groups.

The manifest purpose of the AALS was to create an organization of "forward looking, constructive co-operation of law school teachers, Bar Examiners and the profession," [105] that could protect the public by ensuring the quality of legal education. By 1919, only 48 law schools out of 120 were members of the AALS.[106] Charles Hepburn, an AALS delegate, expressed his concern that "the lower grade law schools are becoming the nurseries of the profession."[107] He complained about how "second-rate schools that exist for revenue only" were gaining ground on the higher grade law schools."[108] The ABA Legal Section and the elite day law school professor members of the AALS joined forces as a juggernaut to increase legal education requirements.[109]

Erwin Griswold, former Solicitor General, and Dean of Harvard supported the AALS because it set higher standards than those promoted by the ABA Legal Education Section.[110] The AALS required its members to develop a minimum of three years of legal study, which was a requirement in place by

[104] Judith Kilpatrick, *Ordinary Men: African-American Lawyers and Civil Rights in Arkansas Before 1950*. 53 ARK. L. REV. 299, 307 (2000).

[105] Id.

[106] *Proceedings of the Section of Legal Education*, 6 A.B.A.J. 64, 81 (1920) (available on Hein Online).

[107] Id.

[108] Id.

[109] Charles Hepburn contended that law school teachers organization (AALS) must cooperate with the ABA's Section of Legal Education to "raise the standards of both pre-legal and legal education." Id. at 82.

[110] Erwin N. Griswold, *Legal Education: 1878–1978*, 64 A.B.A.J. 1051, 1052 (1978).

the time Archer founded his evening school in 1906.[111] The AALS actually lost membership in the aftermath of its three-year minimum study rule because mixed division schools felt that they could not comply with the requirement.[112]

The AALS elite day schools also sought to raise the pre-law educational requirements. In 1900, only three American law schools required any college work, but by 1915, many AALS schools required one or two years of college.[113] The deans of several part-time evening school opposed educational upgrading as "placing the control of legal education ... in the hands of the deans of a few large day law schools."[114] The AALS was also concerned about the problem of unethical conduct by poorly trained night law school graduates who were overcrowding the bar.[115] In actuality, only six of the more than one hundred lawyers disbarred in Massachusetts between 1900 and 1930 were night school graduates.[116] Elite educators asserted that the evening law school education was substandard?

Two deans of AALS schools attributed the problem to the rising tide of lawyers produced by the expanding urban "evening law schools in Boston, New York, Newark, Jersey City, and the District of Columbia."[117] The number of lawyers increased 31 percent from 1920 to 1930, double the growth rate of the U.S. population.[118] Archer's Suffolk was a major cause of the Boston lawyer surplus. Boston's lawyers increased 90% from 1900 to 1930.[119] The AALS sought to impose college training as a condition of law school admission as the most effective contraception against the night schools. The AALS set out to implement that ABA recommendation that part-time schools should require a minimum of four years of extended study.[120] The AALS also maintained that a college degree should be required for law school admission:

> The admission of large number of students who are unable to do good work results either in lowering the standards of the school or else in an

---

[111] Id.

[112] Id.

[113] Id. at 1053.

[114] Id. at 1054.

[115] Young B. Smith & James Grafton Rogers, *The Overcrowding of the Bar and What Can Be Done About It*, 7 AM. L. SCH. REV. 565 (1932).

[116] JOSEPH T. TINNELLY, PART-TIME LEGAL EDUCATION 13 (1957).

[117] Id. at 566.

[118] Id. at 565 (nothing that "there were 122,519 lawyers in 1920 and 160,605 in 1930, an increase of 38,086 or 31 percent, while the increase in population during the same period was only 16 per cent").

[119] Id.

[120] Id at 571 (noting the Association's position "that the required period of study in a part-time school should be extended to four years).

> unnecessary waste of time and money on the part of the incapable students.[121]

These AALS reforms would make it more difficult for evening law schools to compete with day schools which already were beginning to implement these reforms. Archer and evening law schools would be driven to the brink of extinction by the AALS proposal to require law students to hold college degrees. The AALS also sought to stiffen the bar examination requirements. One member noted that fifty percent failure rate for bar examination was a solution to overcrowding.[122]

Gleason Archer organized the evening law schools against the ABA's legal educational section and the educational reformers of the American Association of Law Schools by forming a counter organization, the National Association of Day and Evening Schools (NADELS).[123] Members included historic black schools such as Atlanta Law School, which awarded Archer an honorary doctorate degree, and John Marshall Law School, Chicago's leading evening law school. With the help of his NADELS allies, Archer fought the day law schools on the floor of the American Bar Association Archer portrayed the battle over educational standards as an age-old fight between aristocracy and democracy with its roots in colonial America.[124]

Archer, ever the strategist, proposed resolutions before the ABA that would be popular with the public but that had no hope of passage. In 1927, he called for the ABA to fund undergraduate studies for young men and women, so that the working class could acquire the preliminary education that the day schools felt to be necessary for professional socialization.[125] At the annual dinner of the ABA's Legal Education Section, Archer delivered an address charging that those in charge of the ABA Section were conspiring with the American

---

[121] Id.

[122] Id. at 574 (statement of William Rogers, Esq.)

[123] Michael L. Rustad,. *Turning Carthorses into Trotters: Suffolk Evening Law School as a. Counter-Hegemonic Movement in Legal Education*. 17 THE ADVOCATE 23, 24 (1986) (describing Archer's counter-hegemonic organization of night law schools).

[124] Section Reaffirms Educational Standards for Admission to Bar, 15 A.B.A.J. 795, 798 (1929) (quoting James Brennan, Suffolk Law Graduate) (Note to Syracuse Law Review editors: This is available on Hein Online which your library should subscribe to and you can find this with a search of the most cited U.S. law journals).

[125] Id. at 638 (recommending the "establishment of opportunities for collegiate training, free or moderate costs, so that deserving young and women, seeking admission to the Bar may obtain an adequate preliminary education")

Association of Law Schools to undermine the evening law schools.[126] In a paper entitled "Facts and Implications of College Monopoly of Legal Education," which was read on the opening day of the convention, Archer accused the elite law schools of fostering business for themselves by restricting legal education. He thundered:

> "Now how long are we going to stand for it, gentlemen? How long will we continue to be the dupes of the Association of American Law Schools. ... Only about 30 per cent of the law students of America are being trained in those university schools. Why not give the evening law schools of the country that are bearing the same burden of this thing, some aid, and assistance? My recommendation to you gentlemen is this, that we should clean house in this Section; that we throw out the officials of the Association of Law Schools that have been running this Section ever since they captured it." [127]

Archer succeeded in passing three separate ABA resolutions supporting evening law school interests and also managed to block the day schools' efforts to raise educational requirements for the bar examination.[128] *Time Magazine* reported on the pitched battle between the night law schools led by Archer against the law schools at the 1929 ABA Annual Meetings:

> Educational requirements for admission to the Bar received major consideration and brought in conflict two belligerent factions, one headed by Dean Lewis of Pennsylvania, the other by Dean Gleason Leonard Archer of the Suffolk Law School (Boston night school). Dean Lewis advocated reaffirming the Association's previous recommendation of a two-year college education prior to law study. Dean Archer charged a "clique" within the Association was attempting to foster a "college monopoly on legal education by outlawing evening law schools." Dean Lewis retorted that Dean Archer, in advocating recognition of evening schools, had "commercial interests only." Dean Lewis's recommendation was reaffirmed; law schools operating for profit were condemned.[129]

---

[126] Michael Rustad & Thomas Koenig, *The Impact of History on Contemporary Prestige Images of Boston's Law Schools,* 24 SUFFOLK U. L. REV. 621, 628 (1990) (quoting from ABA Reports of the 1929 meeting of the ABA's Legal Education Section in Memphis Tennessee).

[127] Id. at 639.

[128] Id.

[129] At Memphis, Time Magazine (Nov. 4, 1929) (last visited Sept. 24, 2007), http://www.time.com/time/magazine/article/0,9171,787514,00.html?iid=chix-sphere.

A day school representative charged that the Archer misrepresented the ABA Section's initiatives in his characterization that they were operating as an educational cartel, against the wishes of a majority of the ABA's membership: The exponents of the 'open door,' who believe in 'opportunities for the poor boy' as opposed to qualifications had a full hearing at the last meeting of the Section [ABA Section on Legal Education] in Memphis and were overwhelmed by a vote of greater than ten to one.[130]

Suffolk's Counter-Hegemonic Legal Education Pedagogy

During the 1920s, Suffolk's evening law school employed a black letter law approach to legal education which emphasized frequent testing and review. While Harvard Law professors used the Socratic Method to teach students how to "think like a lawyer," Suffolk students received a more practical education geared to passing the bar examination And local practice. Harvard was training architects of the law whereas Gleason Archer's Suffolk taught the plumbers and the journeymen. The survivors of Suffolk's program could outscore many of Harvard's college men because their courses had been explicitly designed to get them through the examination.

Gleason Archer, the founder of Boston's largest evening law school, Suffolk University Law School, in contrast, wrote simple and direct textbooks. He developed practical guides to over 20 law subjects including torts, contracts, and legal history. Each text was illustrated with many examples drawn from actual practice.[131] Archer stoked the fires of class struggle within the legal profession when he justified the Suffolk method with the claim that: "Under our system a student could learn more law in ten minutes than other students could dig out for themselves in a full day of case reading. This alarmed the people across the Charles and a learned Harvard Overseer once upbraided him for trying to turn "cart horses into trotters." "Of course, he was alarmed for two reasons, we didn't use the case system and we were doing the revolutionary

[130] Will Shaforth, *The Rising Tide of Advocates* , 16 A.B.A.J. 451 (1930). At its first meeting in 1878, the ABA recommended higher standards in legal education. In 1892, the Legal Education Section of the ABA voted that a high school education should be required for admission to the bar (Ames, 1904). However, it was not until 1929 that this became a nationwide requirement. Despite the hard work of the American Association of Law Schools (AALS), the elite law schools' organization, evening schools were more than able to hold their own in pre-Depression America.

[131] GLEASON L. ARCHER, FIFTY YEARS OF SUFFOLK UNIVERSITY, ADDRESS BEFORE THE SUFFOLK LAW SCHOOL ALUMNI ASSOCIATION 1 (1956).

thing of educating boys who were working for a living in the day and studied law at night." [132]

Suffolk Evening Law School's Non-Traditional Students

There is no question that Suffolk admitted a large number of nontraditional students. An African-American graduated in the class of 1915 and a Pequot Indian chief from a Cape Cod tribe graduated in 1925. Throughout the 1920s, articles about the dramatic upward mobility of evening law school graduates appeared in Boston newspapers. Harry Dow, the first Chinese-American admitted to the Massachusetts Bar was a Suffolk graduate. In 1924, he entered Suffolk Law School, attending class in the evening after working by day in his family's laundry. Dean Archer plied the media with Suffolk success stories of poor boys who became lawyers with his help. Another well-publicized success story was that of Isidore Gillman:

> They laughed at Isidore Gillman, Chelsea junkman, but Gillman waited until the last and had a real good laugh-in a full-humored, brand-new lawyer way.
>
> The more they jeered and laughed at me, the more determined I was to make good," said Gillman today. … Gillman, who is thirty-five and who lives at No. 136 Highland Street, Chelsea, was graduated from Suffolk Law School last June after five years of the toughest grind. … At the bar examination he passed with flying colors and all that remains undone now to make him a full-fledged standard bearer of Blackstone is to be sworn in. Ye, who are lame in ambition—or just lazy, listen to Isidore Gillman's story.[133]

Suffolk enrolled students like Eli Levin, who arrived in the United States from Russia just a few years earlier, penniless and not able to speak or understand English. While attending grammar school, Levin washed dishes in a Brookline restaurant on the midnight shift. Later, he was able to obtain a bookkeeping job to sustain him through Suffolk Law School from which he graduated in 1930.[134] Suffolk truly spearheaded the movement of diversity in legal education. Among the early graduates of Suffolk were judges, educators, public officials,

---

132 Id.

133 Author unknown, *Was Junkman. Now is Lawyer*, Boston Evening American (October 28, 1930) at 1.

134 Record (Chelsea) "*Says Yiddish Will Not Die-Eli Levine Worked During His School Days.* (Jan. 8, 1930).

leaders of the fellow men. Early Suffolk graduates served in the Securities and Exchange Commission, The American Federation of Labor, and the Federal Bureau of Investigation. A Suffolk graduate, a native-born Arab, became a professor of law at the University of Iraq in Baghdad.

Suffolk's evening school students were a cross-section of America's working and lower middle class men, who labored during the day as factory workers, baseball players, boxers, police officers, clerks, and newspaper carriers.[135] The Class of 1914, for example, was all male and the median age was above age 30. The reminiscence of George Feingold, former attorney general of Massachusetts, illustrates the flavor of this era:

> At the end of a day's work, I'd hop on one of the trains and ride to North Station. I'd run up Beacon Hill in my overalls with greasy hands. I'd change clothes in the men's locker room in the basement of the Archer Building. I'd wash and change into clean clothes and then run to class. For me, Suffolk Law School was my last hope to make something of myself.[136]

The second graduating class, in 1910, included a glassworker, a letter carrier, a music teacher, a house painter, a clerk, and two sales representatives.[137] James F. O'Brien, a veteran of the Spanish-American War, was a typical student enrolled in Archer's night school.[138] O'Brien financed his legal education by working in a restaurant and supplementing these earning by laboring as a janitor, cleaning Archer's offices.[139] After passing the bar in 1911, O'Brien opened law offices in Fall River and New Bedford, Massachusetts.[140] Thaddeus Alexander Kitchener, an immigrant from Kingston Jamaica and a janitor at Simmons College was a member of Suffolk's Class of 1913.[141] Most students were working class or low-level clerks. Archer's admissions records indicate that the students include shoemakers, farmers, clerks, and bank tellers.[142]

---

135 17 THE ADVOCATE 23 (1986).

136 Interview with the late Richard Jones, Suffolk University Law School conducted by Michael L. Rustad, (March 30, 1984).

137 Suffolk University Archives, *Early Student Research Project, Class of 1912 Profile*, Suffolk University Archives (on file with the authors).

138 Id.

139 Id.

140 Id (quoting from O'Brien's Obituary in the *Fall River Globe*).

141 Beth Bowers, Suffolk University Law School Archives, *Profile of Thaddeus Alexander Kitchener, Class of 1913* (on file with the authors).

142 These records were handwritten records compiled by Gleason Archer at the time the students were enrolled. Limited follow-up data is available on the law students. The data from the class of 1914 was compiled by Suffolk University Archivist Beth Bowers and her staff.

Only half of the 1914 graduates had a high school diploma. Irish-Americans, Jews, and African-Americans were well represented in the early classes. In 1915, Thomas Vreeland Jones was the first African-American to graduate from Suffolk evening law school. Jones worked by day as a superintendent of an office building and became a member of the Massachusetts bar at the age of forty.[143]

Suffolk's Educational Innovations

Christopher Columbus Langdell's scientifically based case system was ill suited to the education of evening law school students who had little prior background in science and no college training. Gleason Archer wrote numerous straightforward textbooks specifically constructed for law students who lacked a good preliminary education. Archer illustrated each of his textbooks with hundreds of problems based upon actual cases or drawn from law office practice.[144] The format of Archer's textbooks resembled the Baltimore Catechism taught to generations of working class Catholics in the form of rote questions and answers.[145]

Archer boasted that the "Suffolk Law School System" had evolved since 1906 and "gradually developed and elaborated" into the "most efficient

---

143 Charles H. Rowell, *An Interview With Lois Maillou Jones* (last visited Feb. 8, 2007), http://xroads.virginia.edu/~ug01/westkaemper/callaloo/mailoujones.html (interview with African-Artist who was the daughter of Thomas Vreeland Jones).

144 Gleason L. Archer, FIFTY YEARS OF SUFFOLK UNIVERSITY, ADDRESS BEFORE THE SUFFOLK LAW SCHOOL ALUMNI ASSOCIATION 1 (1956).

145 Gleason Archer's first book entitled, Law Office and Court Procedure was published by Little, Brown and Co. in 1910. It was a practice-oriented book "confined mostly to the practice in Massachusetts and to those states have a similar system of courts. The last half of the book consists almost entirely of concrete examples in direct and cross-examination." *Book Review of Gleason L. Archer, Law Office and Court Procedure* (1910, 3 ME. L. REV. 188, 188 (1909–1910). Archer published textbooks that he sold to his students on nearly every doctrinal area of that era. Archer's practical textbooks included titles such as THE LAW OF CONTRACTS (1920); THE LAW OF TORTS (1938), DIGEST OF EVIDENCE CASES (1930); THE LAW OF REAL PROPERTY (1927); THE LAW OF EVIDENCE (1930); WILLS AND PROBATE (1925); HISTORY OF THE LAW (1928), THE LAW OF AGENCY (1926); CRIMINAL LAW (1925); and ETHICAL OBLIGATIONS OF THE LAWYER (1910). These titles are just a few listed on Amazon.com (last visited Oct. 8, 2007), (http://www.amazon.com/s/ref=sr_pg_4/103-9652470-3907813?ie+UTF&rs=1000&rh=n). The Baltimore Catechism was used by the Catholic Church from 1885 to 1960s as the leading text on Church doctrine. Baltimore Catechism, Wikipedia (last visited Sept. 26, 2007), http://en.wikipedia.org/wiki/Baltimore_Catechism. The Baltimore Catechism's popularity stemmed from its ability to reach persons of limited education. The Catechism uses question and answers such as: "Who Made the World ? [Answer] God made the world. What is man? [Answer] A. Man is a creature composed of body and soul, and made to the image and likeness of God. BALTIMORE CATECHISM NO. 1 (last visited Oct. 9, 2007), http://www.sacred-texts.com/chr/balt/balt1.htm.

method of teaching law."[146] The "Suffolk Method" taught students black letter law by having his students read his law texts in class, frequent classroom review, and graded homework exercises.[147] Suffolk students were never required to read "text books or notes prior to the class."[148] Students were "expected to bring their texts to class" and to read passages from the text aloud under the professor's guidance.[149] Archer viewed the primary role of the professor to "point out the important vital portions and perhaps give additional illustrations." [150]

Since the entire Suffolk law faculty worked as practitioners, they used many examples from actual cases or law office practice rather than from abstract jurisprudential sources. This practical method was to teach "accurate and positive knowledge"[151] as opposed to the methods of self-discovery taught under Harvard's case law system where "the student gropes blindly in the maze (sic) of technical language and judicial reasoning."[152] Suffolk's pedagogy relied heavily upon review through in-class oral recitation, weekly homework exercises and monthly testing in addition to final examinations. [153] Archer required each professor to devote a minimum of fifteen minutes of every lecture to review. The professor called upon students in an oral quiz covering important principles.[154] Archer argued that the Suffolk method of "persistent review" was clearly superior to the "case system" taught in elite schools, which only tested its students during the final examination period.[155] Frequent testing insured that Suffolk students had mastered "principles previously covered in class." [156]

Gleason Archer carried out a relentless attack on the educational pedagogy of the elite day law schools, which he denounced as the "educational octopus." [157] Harvard University Law School employed full-time professors who wrote law review articles and treatises in addition to their classroom

---

146 Gleason L. Archer, STUDY OF PRINCIPLES A FEATURE OF SUFFOLK LAW SCHOOL SYSTEM 2 (1925) (on file with the authors).

147 Id.

148 Id.

149 Id.

150 Id.

151 Id.

152 Id.

153 Id.

154 Id.

155 Id.

156 Id.

157 GLEASON L. ARCHER, THE EDUCATIONAL OCTOPUS: A FEARLESS PORTRAYAL OF MEN'S EVENTS IN THE OLD BAY STATE (1906–1915).

responsibilities. Roscoe Pound, who began teaching at Harvard Law School in 1910, wrote scores of books and founded a school of legal philosophy called *Sociological Jurisprudence.*[158] In the early 1920s, Pound and Felix Frankfurter completed an empirical study of crime reporting in Cleveland newspapers.[159] Such esoteric research was foreign and repugnant to Archer and his law faculty. Suffolk's faculty in 1928 was composed entirely of practitioners, mostly law graduates of Suffolk evening law school as the table below documents:

In contrast to the legal theorists who taught at Harvard, Suffolk hired part-time faculty to teach subjects such as practice, pleading, deeds, bills and notes, workmen's compensation, wills, and probate and bankruptcy. Suffolk faculty members received most of their income from their day jobs in law offices or working for the courts or nearby government offices. Henry Fielding, who taught both Criminal Law and Agency, also served as an Assistant District Attorney of Suffolk County. Fielding's office at 53 State Street was only a short walk from Suffolk.[160] The 1928 faculty also included a Commissioner of the Industrial Accident Board next door at the State House, an Assistant District Attorney of Suffolk County, and a judge connected with the Equity Division of the Suffolk Superior Court. No Suffolk faculty member other than Gleason Archer and his brother Hiram received his compensation entirely from the law school.[161]

Suffolk's Success on the Bar Examination

The survivors of Suffolk's ruthless program of contest mobility regularly outscored college graduates who had attended day law schools.[162] In the January 1925 bar examination, Suffolk led the list of successful applicants with 35, followed by Boston University with 25, followed by Northeastern (11), Harvard (6) and Georgetown (6), with seven additional admittees from schools outside of Massachusetts. Archer crowed that Suffolk "thus contributed more than one-third of all the successful male candidates."[163] He credited the Suffolk

---

158 Wikipedia, *Roscoe Pound* (last visited Oct, 7, 2007), http://en.wikipedia.org/wiki/Roscoe_Pound.
159 Id.
160 Id. at 26.
161 GLEASON L. ARCHER, SUFFOLK LAW ALUMNI DIRECTORY AND FIVE-YEAR BOOK, NO. 1 (1906–1928) (published by Suffolk Law Alumni Association, Boston, Massachusetts, 1928) (on file with the authors).
162 Gleason L. Archer, "Meeting Propaganda with Facts: Bar Exam Records Disprove YMCA Ads," 1 SUFFOLK BULLETIN 1 (1924).
163 Gleason L. Archer, *Thirty-Five Out of Ninety, January 1925 Bar Examination* 1 (Jan. 1925) (on file with the authors).

method for this astounding record of success in which his grammar school and high school educated students competed well with college-educated men rival institutions:

> Could any testimony more eloquently express the growing efficiency of Suffolk Law School's system of teaching? In spite of a growth unparalleled among law schools, an increase from 591 in February 1920 to over 2,000 students in February 1925, the school, through its constant review work and monthly examinations, has kept that personal touch with its students, impossible under a different system, even in a small school.[164]

In the June 1925 bar examination, 62% of Suffolk Evening Law School applicants passed the bar as compared to 52% for all Massachusetts applicants. Only forty-five percent of the Boston University Law School graduates passed the June bar examination (90 out of 196).[165] Archer frequently prepared special charts highlighting the success of his students on the bar examination versus the men of the YMCA Law School's evening program. He noted that in the 1924 class alone, Suffolk men beat the YMCA by twenty percentage points.[166] In the August 1925 bar examination in Maine, only 26 out of 46 applicants passed, but seven out of the ten of Suffolk men were successful.[167] In the Maine bar examination a year earlier, a Suffolk graduate earned the highest mark and eighty percent of Suffolk graduates passed.[168] Suffolk's success on the bar examination could be explained by its Social Darwinist policy of failing weak students. From 1912 to 1915, roughly 1 in 5 students enrolling in Suffolk evening law school graduated.[169]

The evening "degree mills" were lowering the status of the legal profession because they made no pretension that their pedagogy had the countenance of

---

164 Id.

165 Gleason L. Archer, *Results of June 1925 Bar Exam (Aug. 21, 1925*) (Suffolk University Archives) (on file with the authors).

166 Id.

167 Gleason L. Archer, Spe*cial Message From the Dean, Suffolk Law School* (Sept. 21, 1925) at 1 (noting that of the three Suffolk men who failed, "two of the failures were 'lame ducks' who had failed to graduate from Suffolk")

168 Gleason L. Archer, *Results of June 1925 Bar Examination*, Id. at 2 (reporting August of 1924 Maine bar examination results).

169 This data was computed from the Classes of 1912 to 1915. For these years only 63 out of 283 students enrolled graduated with their class. For the class of 1912, 18 men graduated out of 91 enrolled. Twelve out of eighty students graduated with the class of 1913. In 1914 thirteen out of 45 graduated. By 1915, a third of the enrolled students were graduating. These statistics were compiled from data collected by the Suffolk University Archives' Early Student Project.

ancient tradition. They were training practitioners rather than jurists, legal philosophers, or representatives of a governing class. This was truly rubbing salt into patrician wounds because it gave ammunition to those who were arguing that law was a mere technical skill, which did not deserve a place in the university.

Gleason Archer's Lasting Impact on the Legal Profession

As the economic depression set in, Archer's power declined rapidly. The night law schools were disproportionately impacted by the Depression which made it difficult for night students to pay their law school tuition. Suffolk evening law school's enrollments fell 46% between 1928 and 1932. As Archer's power base evaporated, his enemies pressed the offensive on all fronts. In 1930, the American Judicature Society accused Archer of siphoning off $300,000 a year in tuition. The 1931 ABA Meetings soundly thrashed Archer's resolution to require law professors to have practical training by a vote of 67 to 23. In Massachusetts, graduates of Harvard and Boston University law schools took over bar examination grading. Combined with new "fitness requirements," this change lowered Suffolk's bar pass rate to 16% in 1932. In 1935, the State Board of Tax Appeals filed suit against Suffolk, questioning its eligibility to enjoy a tax exemption. Archer was able to beat off this challenge, but Suffolk enrollment continued to decline throughout the Depression era. Suffolk almost went bankrupt during World War II. In addition, many of the other evening schools collapsed while others upgraded to obtain AALS and ABA accreditation.[170]

Archer and his allies did much to open the legal profession but they never succeeded in undoing the alliance between the ABA and the AALS. In 1948, a Board of Trustees composed largely of his former students fired Archer and banned his texts from the library. With Archer removed from power, Suffolk stopped bucking the trend and began a rapid process of "Harvardization." [171] Suffolk's Board of Trustees draped Archer's official portrait in black and placed it in storage, a symbolic gesture aimed at gaining ABA and AALS accreditation. Full-time faculty drawn from elite day schools displaced the Suffolk Method's

---

170 See Michael L. Rustad,. *Turning Carthorses into Trotters: Suffolk Evening Law School as a. Counter-Hegemonic Movement in Legal Education.* 17 THE ADVOCATE 23, 24 (1986)

171 My colleague Gerard Clark coined this term to refer to the mainstreaming of Suffolk which began with its firing Archer and seeking ABA accreditation.

practitioner professors. The ABA rewarded Suffolk for these reforms with accreditation in 1958. Suffolk was admitted to the AALS in 1977.

What was the lasting impact of Suffolk? Graduating from Suffolk evening law school did not guarantee a legal career. [172] Of the thirteen graduates of the class of 1914, only three found law related work.[173] The occupations of Suffolk alumni included work in banking, hospitality, the medical field, and retail sales. One student became a Justice of Peace, which was at the very bottom of the judicial hierarchy.[174] Of the sixty-seven students admitted in 1915, only twenty-two graduated. Alumni of this class worked in the fields of photography, plumbing, insurance, the watch business, telephone service, and janitorial labor.

Minority graduates of Suffolk Law School were particularly unlikely to find that their Suffolk law degree opened opportunity's door. Louis Eugene Pasco, whose mother was African American and whose father was Mexican, graduated from Suffolk in 1914. Pasco was never able to secure a law position and continued to work as a bank clerk after graduation from Suffolk Law School.[175] Thomas Alexander Kitchener, an African-American, continued to work as a janitor for Simmons College after receiving his Suffolk degree in 1913. Thomas Vreeland Jones continued working in shipping after graduating in 1915 and his World War I Draft Registration Card records him as employed as a janitor.[176] No reliable data exists on how many Suffolk graduates ever worked as lawyers. Boston's newspapers of the era rarely featured stories of Suffolk evening law students unable to find employment as lawyers. Did the junkman, the impoverished Jew, or the Chinese graduate prosper after receiving their degrees? The newspapers do not tell us but the Suffolk Law Alumni Directory as well as obituaries provides the best available data on how much mobility evening law school graduates experienced. The 1928 Suffolk Law Alumni Director surveyed 1,516 graduates, 450 alumni responded and is the best available data point on how Suffolk graduates fared in the job

---

172 Obituary of Ernest Carlson, *Ernest Carlson of Norwood, 93, Retired Electrotyper,* BOSTON HERALD (Mar. 22, 1996) at 062 (reporting that Danish-born decedent graduated from Suffolk Law School after graduating from Norwood High School in 1921 and thereafter working at Norwood Press for 35).

173 Id.

174 Id.

175 *Louis E. Pasco, Suffolk Law School 1914*, Suffolk University Archives, Early Graduate Research Project (on file with the authors).(noting that Louis Pasco was employed as a bank clerk for the National Shawmut Bank of Boston after graduating from Suffolk).

176 *Thomas Vreeland Jones, Suffolk Law School 1915*, Suffolk University Archives, Early Graduate Research Project (on file with the authors).

market.[177] A search of obituaries from New England newspaper archives as well as the 1928 Alumni Directory reveals that not a single Suffolk graduate managed to find work in the State Street firms of Boston's Brahmin community.[178]

Unlike their Harvard counterparts, very few, if any, pre-1928 Suffolk graduates landed lucrative positions in national firms. Most graduates were in the lower branches of the law rather than rendering legal services to Boston Brahmin institutions or national corporations. The differential between the roles played by Suffolk alums and Harvard graduates were even greater than what appears from the self-reporting in the alumni directory. The Alumni Directory of 1928 is skewed in its sampling. No records exist on the 1,066 Suffolk alumni that were not recorded in the directory. It is presumed that the non-respondents likely included a disproportionate number of those alumni not able to find legal jobs.

Conclusion

Fast Forward to 2006, Suffolk's Centennial celebration. As a part of its Centennial Celebration, Suffolk Law School held a high profile conference on *Globalization and the US Law School: Comparative and Cultural Perspectives, 1906-2006*. Speakers at the January 2007 conference included U.S. Supreme Court Justice Ruth Bader Ginsburg; Chief Justice Margaret Marshall of the Massachusetts Supreme Judicial Court; Carl Monk, Esq., executive director of the Association of American Law Schools; and Professor Kjell Å. Modéer of the University of Lund, Sweden. The Globalization of Legal Education Convocation was convened at Suffolk's $70 million building. Suffolk's international graduate programs symbolized Suffolk's transformation from a maverick to a mainstream law school. Suffolk's membership in the AALS legal mainstream was highlighted during Suffolk University Law School's Centennial celebration in the fall of 2006 when former President George H. Bush

---

[177] We acknowledge that responses to the Alumni survey are likely to be skewed in favor of more successful Suffolk alumni as opposed to graduates who were unable to find law-related employment or find limited mobility in business or government careers.

[178] Michael Rustad & Thomas Koenig, *An Empirical Study of a Prestige Image in Transition: Suffolk Law Graduates in Large New England Law Firms* THE ADVOCATE 9, 10 (Fall 1990)(reporting content analysis of the 450 graduates who responded to a 1928 Suffolk Alumni Survey and finding that the "overwhelming majority of respondents were working as solo practitioners, in local politics, in small Boston area businesses, working for New England state government or as federal employees" and never for elite law firms).

addressed distinguished guests that included prominent members of Congress, the judiciary, and the Mayor of Boston. Suffolk University Law School trains a disproportionate number of intellectual property lawyers in the most elite law firms in Boston and around the country. The table below demonstrates Suffolk's dramatic progress in Boston's most elite law firms. Many of the graduates finding elite law placement in the field of intellectual property law worked as patent agents in the day and studied at night in Suffolk's evening division. A number of Boston's leading law firms pay their students to attend Suffolk's evening program with a guarantee of employment after graduation.

Alumni Study of Intellectual Property Specialists in Boston (2006)[179]

Law School Attended	*Lawyers Specializing in Intellectual Property in Boston's Ten Largest Law Firms*
Harvard University Law School	54 (32%)
Suffolk University Law School	48 (29%)
Boston University Law School	27 (16%)
Boston College Law School	27 (16%)
New England School of Law	9 (5%)
Northeastern University School of Law	8 (5%)

Suffolk's alumni are ranked first among Boston's law schools in training lawyers working in the most prestigious boutique law firms specializing in the intellectual property. One out of four lawyers working in the top fifteen boutique law firms were trained at Suffolk.[180] Many of these high-end intellectual property specialists trained in the evening division. Suffolk's growing dominance in intellectual property is emblematic of legal education based upon achievement versus elite family background.

179 This data was compiled with Thomas H. Koenig of Northeastern by doing a content analysis of firm websites. We used Martindale Hubbell's Directory of Lawyers as well as the Massachusetts Lawyer's Weekly ranking of the top Boston law firms to compile the data. Our count included partners as well as associates self-identified as intellectual property lawyers.

180 Professor Koenig and I did a content analysis of the top fifteen intellectual property boutique firms using the Massachusetts Lawyer's Weekly survey of law firms. Suffolk was ranked first among the Boston firms with 92 attorneys (25%) followed by Harvard with 43 (16%).

Gleason Archer first argued that legal education must acknowledge opportunity's open door. The evening law school that once made a Suffolk an untouchable in the law school hierarchy is now its greatest strength. The evening school makes it possible for patent agents to work for the most elite law firms by day and complete their law school training at night. Today's evening division has students with diverse interests in many other branches of the law. Today's evening students tend to work in professional jobs during the day and receive their law school training at night.

As in Archer's day, the evening student does "double duty" which is the hard day's night. All of the non-traditional students have brought fantastic diversity thereby transforming American legal education and enriching the practice of law with new insights. Given the high quality of today's evening students and their law success upon graduation in Suffolk and other law schools, it is clear that Archer achieved his goal of diversifying the legal profession. Archer's efforts enabled those who must work to support their families or who simply desire to maintain their professional career while attending school to achieve their goal of receiving a solid legal education. He was a progressive, innovative, and influential figure in American legal education. Archer's challenge to the legal profession's exclusion of the evening law schools forever changed the path of legal education. As Hegel reminds us, "When philosophy paints its gray in gray, then has shape of life grown old. By philosophy's gray in gray, it cannot be rejuvenated but only understood. The owl of Minerva spreads its wings only with the falling of the dusk."[181]

[181] Georg Hegel, Philosophy of Right.

Kjell Å. Modéer

Theory and Practice or Practice without Theory? Legal Education in Sweden in the Time of the Progressive Era

1. Comparing Legal Education in Time and Space

The 20th century has been called "Law's century". If it's so, it can to a great extent also be regarded as "Lawyer's century". The educated and trained lawyer played an instrumental role for the development of the modern society of the 20th century in Europe as well as in the U.S. In *civil law*-countries in continental Europe of the 19th century France and later Germany demonstrated the need for a codification and for modern legal science as catalysts for the transformation of the traditional European national state into a modern one. American legal history demonstrates how important these legal sources also were for the American legal discourses. Also in small European countries like Sweden this transition has been significant and substantial. The institutions for legal education e.g. have increased from two (Uppsala and Lund) in 1906 to ten in 2006.[1]

Historians love to show the new is old, Laura Kalman noted in a recent article. "It is one of our favourite parlor games. We take what someone (often a sociologist, political scientist, or lawyer) has identified a recent problem and demonstrate it predates time."[2] Comparing times is commonplace for all lawyers. In this article I will try to expand my comparison also to space. One century ago the influences from German legal culture, legal science and legal education were great in the U.S. as well as in Sweden. So my task will be to map up how Swedish legal education in the beginning of the 20th century fitted into a pattern of European models, especially the German one.

---

1 Masters of Law (jur. kand.) exams can be taken at Uppsala, Lund, Stockholm, Umeå, Gothenburg and Örebro University. Masters of business law etc. can be taken at Linköping, Jönköping, Luleå and Karlstad.

2 Laura Kalman, Professing Law: Elite Law School Professors in the Twentieth Century. In: Austin Sarat, Bryant Garth & Robert A. Kagan (ed.), Looking Back at Law's Century, Cornell University Press: Ithaca & London 2002, 337.

In 1906 we are celebrating the centenary of Suffolk School of Law, inaugurated by Gleason L. Archer in 1906, in Louis Brandeis' Boston in the midst of the progressive era, in the context of *Lochner* and the importance of this Supreme Court landmark decision, which highly supported the development of the corporative lawyer and the elitist American Bar Association.

I will compare the legal education and training at the new-erected Suffolk Law School with that in Sweden in the beginning of the 20th century. Making such a comparison it's important to take the relevant levels of comparison. You have to compare the American legal education with the Continental European and that of Massachusetts with the Swedish—or at least the geographical American North-East with the European North: the Scandinavian countries.

The progressive era in the U.S. is to compare with the embryonic time for the European social state or welfare-state. The period from around 1870 up to the Great War can be described as the time of European *pre-modernity.* After the French-German War the Second German Empire in 1870 became not only a political but also in a wider sense a cultural model for many European as well as non-European countries. Within law German legal science got a high esteemed reputation, especially the intellectual grand children to Friedrich Carl von Savigny, the founder of the Historical School of law, became the instrumentalists for legal reform, when the pre-modernity grew into the modernity of the 20th century.

2. Suffolk vs. Harvard in 1906

The year of 1906 is, as this article will indicate, an important year not only in American legal history, but also in the German, and in the Swedish. The years around the turn of the century 1900 brought optimism and enthusiasm to the law schools. Development was the term of the day. Lawyers were increasingly trained to be social engineers in a time of reform.

In the United States the creation of the private Suffolk Law School was one example of the reaction against the "Harvardization" of American legal education.[3] Already in 1886 Oliver Wendell Holmes had taken stand to Christopher Columbus Langdell's case method and embraced its "scientism".

---

[3] Michael L. Rustad, Turning Cart Horses into Trotters: Suffolk Evening Law School as a Counter Hegemonic Movement in Legal Education, 17 The Advocate No. 2, [The Suffolk University Law School Journal] Spring 1986, 18 ff; Michael L. Rustad & Thomas Koenig, The Impact of History on Contemporary Prestige Images of Boston's Law Schools, 24 Suffolk University Law Review (1990) No. 3, 621 ff. Michael L. Rustad, A Hard Day's Night, in this volume, 25 ff.

It was, so Holmes, “to teach in the grand manner and to make lawyers”. The case method was closely related to “the influence of German science”. German theoretical views were transformed into the great American pedagogical creation, *the case method.*[4]It meant that it was “gradually drawing legal history into its sphere.”[5] But it was also easy for Holmes to translate “the scientific search for rules into a scientific analysis of facts”. In that respect he was an early legal realist![6]

More generally Gleason L. Archer’s evening law school was a reaction against the “law in book”-concept. The modern realistically orientated law school was more devoted to “law in action” than to “law in books”. Roscoe Pound, who later for two decades should be the Dean of Harvard Law School, in his famous lecture at the ABA-meeting in St. Paul 1906 heavily attacked the formal and doctrinal American legal establishment and gave the national Bar advice about “What Constitutes a Good Legal Education”.[7] Some years later he provoked the legal educators stating they were “legal monks”. Pound pioneered in pleading for interdisciplinary perspectives within the law. Training in politics, economics and sociological jurisprudence was necessary to “fit new generations of lawyers to lead the people”.[8]

In that respect and in that context the creation of the Suffolk Law School in 1906 was a landmark event in American legal history. Its founder, the 26 years old Gleason L. Archer, created a provocative alternative to the Harvard model. Archer opened an Evening Law School at his home in Roxbury to “serve ambitious young men who are obliged to work for a living while studying law”.[9] This anti-elitist project, devoted to promote the encouragement of the “unworthy” poor, had social and political aims. Archer saw two main dangers in the society: the “reds” (Communists) and the “crimsons” (Harvard). He wanted to struggle against these two sinister forces in the society. His course was therefore highly practical. The pedagogical technique was that of a lecturer dictating notes. His law school became a success-story. Two decades later,

---

4 Filippo Ranieri, Juristen für Europa: Wahre und falsche Probleme in der derzeitigen Reformdiskussion zur deutschen Juristenausbildung, Juristen Zeitung 1997, 801 ff.

5 Oliver Wendell Holmes, The Use and Meaning of Law Schools, and Their Methods of Instruction, 1886, 919, 922.

6 Robert Stevens, Law School: Legal Education in America from the 1850s to the 1980s, The University of North Carolina Press: Chapel Hill & London 1983, 122 f.

7 Roscoe Pound, The Causes of Popular Dissatisfaction with the Administration of Justice, 29 A.B.A.R. 395, 397 (1906).

8 Stevens, (1983), 134.

9 Michael Rustad, [Footnote 3], David L. Robbins, Suffolk University: A History of Suffolk University 1906–1996, Boston 1996, 11.

Archer proudly claimed that Suffolk was the largest school of law in the world, with nearly 4,000 students.[10]

The legal contexts of Boston in 1906 were full of conflicts: Suffolk vs. Harvard meant competition between law schools. Idealistic—and practically—orientated law schools competed with well established and scientifically orientated elitist law schools. It was also a struggle between the poor vs. the rich, and the reformers vs. the Tocquevillian aristocracy. The organisation of legal aid societies—The Boston Legal Aid Society was founded in 1900—indicated the need to protect the weaker parties in legal life and transformed successively from charity to substantive legal reform.[11]

3. Swedish Legal Education: Traditional Faculties vs. Metropolitan Faculty

At the turn of the century 1900 also the Swedish law faculties were involved in a competition between the universities. The oldest university in Uppsala was also the bigger one. At Uppsala about 400 students studied the law, in Lund there were about 125.[12] The students moved from one university to the other. They went where it was easiest to take the exam. The threat to most of the law professors at the two faculties, however, was the plans to institute a quite new law faculty in Stockholm. The proposal to create a law faculty in the nation's capitol was made in parliamentarian discussions already in 1856–58 and had since then been an ongoing discourse. One suggestion had been to move the law faculty in Uppsala to Stockholm, another to close down not only the faculty of law at Uppsala but also that of Lund to establish a national faculty in the capitol.[13] This proposal to establish new universities in the capitols had turned out to be a European trend in the 19th century. It started with the famous Prussian Reform University in Berlin 1810 and with the University of Christiania (Oslo) in Norway 1811. It continued with the foundation of universities in S:t Petersburg in Russia 1819, in London 1828, in Brussels 1834 and in Athens 1836.[14]

The great benefit with such a metropolitan institution should be a better

---

[10] Stevens (1983), 80.

[11] Mark NMI Spiegel, The Boston Legal Aid Society: 1900 – 1925, Massachusetts Legal History, vol.9, 2003.

[12] Professor John Adolf Ask, Lund University, Faculty of law, Minutes 18.4.1894, A 1A:12.

[13] S.R.D. Knut Olivecrona, Om den juridiska undervisningen vid Universitetet i Upsala och om den juridiska fakultetens förflyttande till Stockholm, 2 uppl., Upsala 1859, 87 f.

[14] Olivecrona (1859), 99.

interaction "between school and life, between theory and practice"—between knowledge and experience.[15] The connection to practical life should be a new phase in the development of the universities. The law professor Knut Olivecrona in Uppsala, however, was sceptical to this argument. In 1859 four of his Uppsala colleagues were already engaged with heavy obligations within public committees. Even if the law professors certainly would be more used in such committees if they were located at Stockholm, he questioned if that would be a good solution for the universities as a whole, if the result was that the students missed their professors.

Another comparison was made with the post-napoleon French law faculties. It was, however, regarded as a bad model. The French way to split up the universities and then construct a "special faculty" was in Sweden regarded as a frightening model.[16] As a part of a university the law faculty traditionally cooperated with the philosophical faculty. History, statistics, philosophy, classical philology, Old Norse linguistics and archaeology were necessary and basic sciences for mature legal studies, it was argued. Forensic medicine affiliated the law faculty with the medical faculty, and ecclesiastic law with the theologian. Scientific universality developed an independence and freedom, which should be totally spoiled if the law faculties at the universities were broken out from the scientific orientated universities to be "a school of applications for judges and other civil servants to be".[17] Olivecrona made five arguments against the proposal: 1) The stimulating effect of competition between the faculties disappeared; 2) the disciplines of history and philosophy—which were the important disciplines within contemporary legal science—should be weakened or even abolished; 3) the academic freedom would be succeeded by a more primitive school-like education without any scientific touch; 4) the legal education should get an narrow-minded practical direction, theoretical studies should be pushed aside to give priority to practical skills; 5) it would all result in an increasing difficulty to find the able teachers to such an institution.

The parliamentarians, however, looked upon the legal education given at the old Swedish law faculties as one-sided "theoretical", "inapplicable for practical life", and the subjects of the lectures given to the students were regarded as "insignificant for jurists". Olivecrona, however, defended the state of the art: It was the duty of the law faculties to give the students such a scientific

---

15 Olivecrona (1859), 103.
16 Olivecrona (1859), 124.
17 Olivecrona (1859), 125.

grounding so they later on with success could enter their practical careers. It was their obligation to educate scientifically well educated jurists. The law faculties had a higher aim to fulfil than just to give a special education for the practical civil servants. In Uppsala, Olivecrona stated, the students got a legal education with the purpose to educate them to "citizens".[18] In his wide argumentation he also quoted Blackstone's view regarding the law student: "If practice be the whole he is taught, practice must also be the whole he will ever know." To sum up this part: The questioning of theoretical studies of law was an effect of the increasingly scientific legal education, to a great extent due to influences especially from Germany and the Historical school of jurisprudence. More generally it created an increasing alienation between the law faculties and the courts, between the law professors and the judges. In the long run it resulted in concrete conflicts about the aim of the legal education.

4. "Strugglers" for Legal Education

Within European legal culture during the three decades from 1870 up to the 20th century one important keyword became *professionalisation* with help of state regulation. The legal actors dominated the social arenas. The judge was regarded as a king, *Richterkönig*, the modern lawyer, who protected the individual citizen in the *Rechtsstaat* was born, Bar associations were founded, and as legal conflicts increased in this modern society new courthouses were constructed as sacred temples of the law in which legal problems could be solved. In this context of reforms the old-fashioned and traditional legal education came in focus. The Swedish law faculties were understaffed, the curriculum, the models of teaching and examination as well as the law degrees were criticised from outside the university and regarded as outdated. Claims for reforms came both from practitioners and politicians from outside the university but also from the law professors themselves. The concrete initiative to reform the legal education was taken by the faculty of law at Uppsala in 1891. The faculty directed a petition to the Government to reform the law degree and the examination system.[19] This petition resulted in a decade-long investigation and discourse and ended up the new study reform 1904.

Many Scandinavian jurists with ambitions to end up as law professors made their pilgrimage to German universities to study the educational reforms in the

---

[18] Olivecrona (1859), 129.

[19] Nytt Juridiskt Arkif II 1892, no 4, 1 ff. – Christian Häthén, Legal Education in Sweden During 1870 – 1930, In: Från Schlyters Lustgård. Rättshistoriska uppsatser 1:2001, 76 ff.

increasingly merging Second Empire. This generation of Scandinavian law reformers and law professors at the end of the 19th century could be appointed to be the "Strugglers for the Law". They were to a great extent inspired by a Darwinist approach to the law demonstrated by the German legal scholar, Rudolph von Jhering. His ideas and works have been of great importance not only for the Swedish but also for American judges and law professors. Jhering opened up a quite new perspective for the German jurists. Trained in the extremely doctrinal and theoretical legal environment of the Historical School (Windscheid) Jhering increasingly looked upon his colleagues as sitting in an ivy tower without any connection to legal realities and to the judicial world outside their theoretical jurisprudential chambers. He called upon a more international and practically orientated legal science. For the modernization of German legal education Jhering was a catalyst. He tried to eliminate the increasing gap between theory and praxis by introducing practical training as a part of the scientific legal education. His course material for the legal education, *"Daily Life Jurisprudence"* (Jurisprudenz des täglichen Lebens), was regarded as an introductory preliminary school for the legal view of the reality.[20]

Already the title of Jhering's famous lecture in Vienna 1872, *The Struggle for Law* (*der Kampf ums Recht*) referred to the discourses on development theories articulated by Darwin (*Struggle for Life*). It was also an articulated plea to oppose German legal formalism. Jhering consciously addressed the practitioners, the judiciary and the lawyers. His lecture was translated into many languages, and it was widely circulated and became a most read contribution also to a younger generation of idealistically orientated legal scholars—and practitioners. In the U.S. there are great similarities between Oliver Wendell Holmes' approach and Jhering's. It's evident that Holmes read Jhering's English version while he worked on *The Common Law.* If he right understood Jhering's concept and views is however another question.[21]

In the 1880's several Scandinavian scholars converted into Jhering's new legal religion.[22] Jhering's lecture was translated into Swedish by Ivar Afzelius,

---

[20] Rudolf Leonhard, Hovedstrømningerne i den nyere tyske Retsvidenskab, 10 Tidsskrift for Retsvidenskab (1897), 132 f.

[21] Mathias W. Reimann, The Common Law and German Legal Science, In: Robert W. Gordon (ed.), The Legacy of Oliver Wendell Holmes, Jr., Stanford University Press: Stanford 1992, 102.

[22] In Denmark Viggo Bentzon, Ditlev Tamm, Det rets- og statsvidenskabelige fakultet, Københavns universitet 1479 – 1979, Bind VI.1, Københavns universitet: København 2005, 271 ff. and in Norway Francis Hagerup, Sten Gagnér, Hagerups tidskrift, Tidsskrift for Retsvidenskab 1999, 255 ff.

a law professor in Uppsala who reluctantly had adopted his ideas.[23] More enthusiastically it was received for example by Alfred Ossian Winroth, from 1892 professor of private law at Lund University. His inaugural lecture this year was titled: *Legal Theory and Practice*.[24] It was an academic sermon based on the Jhering gospel.

Winroth was an extraordinary "Struggler for the Law". Like Jhering he started out his academic career in the 1880's as holder of a professorship in legal history at Lund, which he left when he got the chair in private law. The minutes from the faculty meetings in the 1890's regularly reported about his consequent and uncompromising struggles with his colleagues. "If I was the king" was the antecedent clause he normally used, when he explained how he should have acted if he was a legislator. "It was obviously not as a king in a parliamentarian kingdom" he wanted to reign, one of his colleagues noted in a tribute after his death. "I doubt he hadn't been satisfied until he had been a Genghis Khan, the king of the kings. His commanding attitude was reflected in his by no means female look, which occasionally almost induced the mind to an autocrat." When he during a vacation went to a European spa and there mingled with the high society, the guardians were amazed when the learnt that this man was a university professor from Lund and not a king from some distant reign.[25]

Winroth held his inaugural lecture in the sacred lecture hall of the new university building in Lund, inaugurated in 1882 in a classical Greek style as a European temple of science. "A society is born in struggle and unrest is an old observation", he stated. "Is a cause good, why then waste words?" He was not interested in the good side, he wanted to focus on lacks and faults. He pleaded for reforms in the future. "If you are not going forward you are sliding downhill. It's development's law." This rhetoric Darwinist prologue of his lecture brought him to the lacks and faults within the judicial system. Theory and praxis had to be regarded as the two sides of the same coin. The law professor had "To know and [how] to bring knowledge to application." In Sweden there was a gulf between theory and praxis, he stated. Like Germany also Sweden had to reform its old code from 1734. The experience to learn

[23] Ivar Afzelius, Striden för rätten, Stockholm 1879; Kjell Å Modéer, Jherings Rechtsdenken als Herausforderung für die skandinavische Jurisprudenz, In: Claes Peterson (ed.), Juristische Theoriebildung und Rechtliche Einheit. Beiträge zu einem rechtshistorischen Seminar in Stockholm im September 1992, Rättshistoriska studier, Band 19, Lund 1993, 91 ff.

[24] A. Winroth, Juridisk teori och praxis. Föreläsning vid installation den 19 september 1892, Lund 1892.

[25] Johan C.W. Thyrén, Akademiska tal (1888–1915), Lund 1916, 128.

from Germany was that a modern codification had to rely on theory. A reform needed neither practitioners who themselves acquired a greater legal knowledge nor a greater support from "the guardians of legal science", the law professors. Especially the lack of knowledge in legal history caused problems for the legislators. "They don't have eyes for the mind and spirit of our legal system and for uniting legal principles." They don't know how to handle separate legal clauses in creating a systematic legislation. Their lack of theory makes them turn down the history and instead focus on foreign modern legal systems. And it takes a lot of time to realize that foreign rules don't fit into our system. So Winroth blamed the legislators. They worked too slowly; the result was poor and not national. The reason was the lack of theoretical education among the legislators.

An educational reform towards more theory of course had to start out from the universities. The law professors had to get a better position in the society. "If theory should achieve what it ought to do, it had to be represented at the universities by its most outstanding members." And they, on the other hand, had to include material from praxis in their legal education. If it was a wish from the practitioners for "more theory", Winroth argued, they on the other side could call the theorists for "more praxis". Personal cooperation became his keyword. The Court of Appeal for southern Sweden was founded in 1820 and was located to an old garrison town Kristianstad, once upon a time a famous and well reputed garrison town but in times of modernization it had increasingly got a marginalized location. Winroth saw the solution: Move the Court of Appeal to Lund and use the appellate judges as legal educators, and correspondingly the law professors as adjunct judges. "But if not the mountain will go to Mohammed, Mohammed has to go to the mountain". Winroth didn't suggest that the law faculty in Lund should move to Kristianstad. His reference was the ongoing—and increasingly actual—plans to establish a new faculty of law in Stockholm. It may seem odd that the new professor stood in the rostrum of the lecture hall at Lund and like a traitor declared he was an enthusiastic advocate of such plans. But he added: "Lund, though, is not threatened by danger. It will remain as the outpost of the nation to the continental Europe; the place which first hand will receive thoughts and movements from the educational breeding grounds of the rest of civilized people."[26] Legal science, however, also needed a relation to Swedish legal praxis, and for this purpose Stockholm should be the right place for a "powerful and vivid law faculty",

[26] Winroth (1892), 30.

complementary to Uppsala and Lund, but located in the focal point of Swedish legal practice. The law professors at Stockholm had in the future to cooperate with the practitioners, their proposals wouldn't fall on deaf ears, and their works wouldn't be treated as unwritten. Legal theory and praxis would at last be combined in an optimal way.

Winroth's manifesto was read with surprise by a former colleague of his at Uppsala, Ivar Afzelius. Afzelius considered that Winroth to a great extent battered at open doors. Afzelius himself had left a position as law professor at Uppsala to be a member of the Swedish High Court, so he was himself an example of the mobility from theory to praxis. The old antagonism between theorists and practitioners had in his views disappeared. Arguing from his position as a practitioner, Afzelius felt, that theoretical merits were well regarded in judicial careers. But he totally agreed with Winroth that the theoretical foundation of the legal education still determined the practitioner's way to see and act.[27]

5. Theory or Practice in Legal Teaching

Again, as we heard Winroth didn't prefer the road of compromise. He struggled permanently, especially with his colleagues in the faculty. One important struggle occurred in 1894 when the principal question was put how to administer the legal education in the future.[28] Traditionally the Swedish legal teaching was divided into public lectures and private tutorials (kollegier). The public lectures were open to the public, to get access to the private tutorials arranged by the professors the students had to pay a fee. At the seminars the professors went through the most important parts of the field, important with respect of the examination. The private education in those courses was very "concentrated and close to school teaching" (Hamilton). There were no printed course books, so it was difficult for the students to pass the exam if they hadn't participated in the professor's tutorials. The public lectures, on the other hand, dealt with more theoretical (and scientific) parts of the field. Normally just a few students were registered to those public events. The faculty minutes show that this division between theory and practice, between free of charge and fee-based education created problems and were regularly under debate.

[27] I[var] A[fzelius], Anm. Af Winroth, Juridisk teori och praxis, 6 Tidsskrift for Retsvidenskab (1893), 129 ff.

[28] Lund University, Faculty of Law, Minutes 18.4.1894, A 1A:12.

Winroth attacked one of his colleagues for having at the same time given on one hand three tutorial-based courses and on the other hand totally irrelevant and unimportant public lectures for 4 students. Winroth had visited one of his colleague's boring and dogmatic lectures. He found a professor of law dictating a manuscript slowly to his students. Winroth observed that the lecture apparently was based on some German reference-book. It was a scandal, he said, that the professor, paid by the state, didn't adjust his public lectures to topics of relevance for the upcoming generation of judges, and instead directed them to take elementary information at the fee-paid tutorials preparing for the exam.

Winroth's sharp and concrete criticism regarding one of his colleagues, ended up with claims for a reform not only regarding the legal education and the curriculum but also alternative forms for examination. He suggested an external commission like that introduced in Germany. He also claimed the need for printed course-material. In his views it was a scandal that his colleagues not had given priority to write new course-books—especially for the private tutorials. The faculty minutes still give you a glimpse of the charged mood around the faculty table. There were colleagues who objected, other who tried to compromise, also other who found Winroth's criticism well-founded. Winroth's proposal regarding a German-like examination system was declined, but regarding publishing the notes from law lectures the Swedish government in 1900 introduced an annual grant for this purpose. One of the first applicants for such a grant were the Law Students' Associations at Lund and Uppsala, who both applied for publishing of professor Winroth's lectures on Swedish property law![29]

6. European Reforms in Legal Education

All these dreams to combine theory and practice, however, couldn't be realized if not a legal educational reform took place. In the decade to come, between 1894 and 1904, legal educational reform became a big discourse throughout Europe. In Germany the legal culture was totally reformed during this decade. The creation and implementation of the German civil code, *Bürgerliches Gesetzbuch*, 1896–1900 totally reformed the legal education. Also Scandinavian legal scholars followed closely this transition.[30] The Danish law professor

[29] Faculty of Law, Minutes 2.2.1901, § 49.

[30] F[rancis] H[agerup], Det juridiske Studiums ordning [i Tyskland], 9 Tidsskrift for Retsvitenskab (1896), 349 f.

Viggo Bentzon returned in 1900 from a study tour to Germany. He was inspired to reform the legal education at Copenhagen more like the German into "a less dogmatic and more concrete-practical legal education".[31] The reformation of the German legal education and examination started with the new procedural laws for the Second Empire adopted already in 1877.[32] To be a judge, a prosecutor, lawyer or Notar—e.g. to be a holder of a higher position as civil servant—you had to take to exams, the first after at least three years of study, and the second after at least three years of practical work in a court or at the offices of the prosecutor or at a law-firm. Alfred Winroth, who himself had once served as a judge for some years in the 1880's, was evidently inspired by this German form of interaction between theory and practice. The German model became still more important in 1900. The new civil code not only made the examinations much more homogeneous all over Germany, as the particular laws in the states were abolished and were substituted by the new code. It also created a more general curriculum, which started with jurisprudence (allmän rättslära) and continued with Roman and German legal history. The Roman and German foundations of private law should be emphasized in two preparatory courses.[33]

The spirit of the legal revolution in 1900 in Germany, accomplished by legislators and law professors and implemented by the judges, also enlightened the Swedish law professors. Scandinavian legal culture was passionate for German legal culture. Even the American legal literature had to be translated into German to be read by Scandinavian jurists. When Oliver Wendell Holmes' book *The Common Law* in 1912 was translated into German, a Scandinavian law journal in a review indicated that it was to prefer to read the German translation "which helps [the reader] past the difficulties the many curious English legal *termini technici* present".[34]

7. Swedish Reform in Legal Education 1904

At the Lund Faculty of Law there was around 1900 a shift of generation. Professor Winroth left for Uppsala, other left due to age and some new talented professor took their seats. I need to mention some. Winroth's successor was the professor of legal history at Lund Carl G.E. Björling, who also was deeply

[31] Viggo Bentzon, De juridiske Eksaminer i Tyskland og Danmark, Ugeskrift for Retsvaesen (1900), 657 ff. – Ditlev Tamm (2005), 271 f.
[32] Gerichtsverfassungsgesetz 27.1.1877, § 2.
[33] F.H. (1896), 349 f.
[34] F. Hagerup, Anm. av Dr. O.W.Holmes Jr., Das gemeine Recht Englands und Nordamerikas, 25 Tidsskrift for Retsvidenskab (1912), 313.

engaged in the legal educational reform. In 1900 he had published an extensive survey regarding the reformation of the Finnish legal education and examination.[35] Even if you don't have to remember the names of this new generation you can't resist their faces. Johan Thyrén, professor of penal law, for decades the reformer of Swedish penal law, and one of Winroth's sympathizers regarding legal educational reforms, was a devoted admirer of the German sociological school of penal law and a pioneer in offering the students printed course books. The students gave his book in penal law a popular name, "*The Green Danger*" (Gröna faran), which indicated that his public lectures still were too scientific for the students. Another colourful and controversial law professor was Knut Wicksell, the first holder of a professorship in economics and financial law, and before Keynes a very famous representative of modern economic theories. Wicksell came as a radical outsider to Lund from Uppsala. His political utterances brought him in conflict with the contemporary establishment, but he belonged to the liberals regarding the legal education.[36] His professorship indicated another trend within the discourses regarding legal education: Interdisciplinarity.

In Denmark the new study reform with new exams—inspired by the German—was taken in 1902. Also this reform was to a great extent inspired by German discourses. In Germany economics had been the field to introduce the law students about the society in which the legal rules were working. This form of "Rechtstatsachenforschung" was also stimulated by the contemporary discourses on sociology with Max Weber and Eugen Ehrlich as important participants. On the other hand the Danish educational reform indicated a decline of scientific elements and an increase of practice. In a new practical course with "Concrete Questions" (Konkret Opgave) the students had to solve practical legal problems, evidently inspired by Jhering's concept.[37]

The same year the Danish reform was accomplished a corresponding initiative was taken in Sweden. Ernst Trygger, law professor at Uppsala and later also member of the High Court, presented a motion in the parliament, which raised the problems within the legal education and examination. General knowledge could be important but professional studies were still more important. General knowledge should be a requisite for the entrance to the legal education. The high schools (gymnasium) should in the future bring the

[35] Carl G.E.Björling, Finnlands juridiska examensväsende, Review: Studier och examina i Juridiska fakulteten, Helsingfors 1899, 13 Tidsskrift for Retsvidenskab (1900), 149 ff.
[36] Torsten Gårdlund, Knut Wicksell. Rebell i det nya riket, Bonniers 1956, 236 ff.
[37] Ditlev Tamm (2005), 272.

general knowledge to the law students to be. If this change could be implemented the old-fashioned degree system with preliminary exams could be abolished.[38]

Two years later, in 1904, the new study ordinance was adopted and implemented at the Swedish faculties of law. The ordinance regarded the heavy criticism from the late 19th century and introduced a new degree system with only one degree, the juris kandidat exam. Regarding the curriculum instead of preliminary exams an introductory, propedeutic course in private law with central elements of penal law and law of procedure became compulsory. The new trend with more realistic fields of study was also realized as the Swedish law students from now on, like in Denmark, had to take a compulsory course in "professional practice".

Latin was still a requisite for law studies but the students didn't any longer had to take a compulsory course in Roman law. This field was regarded as broader knowledge and could be substituted by economics. When the proposal to this reform was discussed within the law faculty at Lund professor Björling made objections to make Roman law an optional field. "Roman law is necessary for a qualified law degree which should guarantee a solid education for the judges to be." He pointed out how Roman law still was an important compulsory field in the legal education in Germany, France and England. Björling also emphasized the need for knowledge in German. He urged, that skills in German language had to be a requisite for legal studies. "With the importance German literature has for our culture and also for our legal system, knowledge in German language must be indispensable for a Swedish jurist."[39] This aim for Germanization of the legal culture and legal science dominated Swedish jurists up to the Second World War.

8. The Year 1906 as a Starting Point for New Trends in Legal Culture

In 1906 the legal education was reformed in USA, in Germany as in Sweden. In 1906 Roscoe Pound started his crusade away from what he regarded as "mechanical jurisprudence" in direction towards a sociological jurisprudence and wrote his Manifesto of what constitutes a good legal education. In this social and economical contextualization of the law Louis Brandeis in *Muller*

[38] Christian Häthén, (2001), 80 f.

[39] C.G. Björling in Faculty of law, Minutes 28.10.1903, § 115.

v. Oregon 1908 introduced the "Brandeis Brief" this new sociological and empirical trend.

In Germany the young jurist Hermann Kantorowicz also argued for sociology as an important part of legal science. "Dogmatic without legal science is empty, sociology without dogmatic is blind", was one of his famous statements. In 1906 Kantorowicz published his Manifesto of the Free Law Movement, *Struggle for the Legal Science* (*Kampf um die Rechtswissenschaft*) which connected all the minds of those German legal scientists from Rudolf von Jhering to Eugen Ehrlich, who both had argued against the dogmatic and formal way of law.[40] Ehrlich had already in 1903 proclaimed the German struggle for new legal methods,[41] and now both of them identified and acted for a "free law doctrine" which saw the gaps in the law, and which needed to be filled with judge-made law. The manifesto was an imperative to the practitioners of law, just like Jhering's manifesto was some 30 years earlier: "Attention all judges and lawyers" was the author's outcry in the preface.[42] This antithesis to the legal positivists legal concept played a substantial role in German legal discourses up to the 1930's.

Interestingly enough the "free law doctrine" didn't play any substantial role in Swedish German-inspired legal science. From the turn of the century 1900 Sweden—like the dominant German doctrine—in legal science as well as in legal education applied the positivist and later the realist method. The anti-metaphysical legal realism started out from Uppsala in the 1910's and turned up as the *Scandinavian legal realism,* which dominated three generations of Swedish jurists. In 1906 one of the main academic discourses in Sweden came to an end when the board of Stockholm College, later Stockholm University, decided to create six professorships in law. One year later, in the fall of 1907, 81 law students matriculated at the so called Political- and Law Faculty at Stockholm and started their legal education.[43] Let's now return to Alfred Ossian Winroth. In 1906 this restless mind after six years left his professorship at Uppsala, and ended his career as the first professor of private law at the law faculty in Stockholm. Also in Stockholm he held his inaugural lecture on the

---

40 Hermann Kantorowicz, Rechtswissenschaft und Soziologie, 1911, New printing 1962, 139.

41 Eugen Ehrlich, Freie Rechtsfindung und freie Rechtswissenschaft, 1903; Stephan Meder, Rechtsgeschichte 2.ed., Böhlau UTB Köln/Weimar/Wien 2005, 346 ff.

42 Frank Kantorowicz Carter, Gustav Radbruch and Hermann Kantorowicz: Two Friends and a Book – Reflections on Gnaeus Flavius' *Der Kampf um die Rechtswissenschaft,* 7 German Law Journal (2005), 657 ff, 663.

43 Åke Hassler, Om fakultetens tillkomst och verksamhet, in: Minnesskrift utgiven av Juridiska fakulteten i Stockholm vid dess femtioårsjubileum 1957, P.A.Norstedts Förlag Stockholm 1957, 281 f.

judicial system and legal education.[44] This time Winroth didn't blame the badly educated legislators. Now Winroth focused on the ignorant judge who emphasized on formalism and was stuck in his docket of cases. "The judge doesn't know how to judge". But the ignorance was not his guilt or responsibility but the legal education, he said. The aim of the legal education had to be to create parts of the social machines, which had to be adjusted to their future place in the public institutions, where they could do a god job. Professional education really has to be professional, and the general knowledge has to be a part of life and left to the responsibility of the individual. Winroth again made a forceful plea for academic freedom. The ordinance of 1904 had too stringently regulated the studies of law. He argued for more of optional courses in the curriculum.

9. Conclusion: European State Control vs. American Educational Market

Let me try to conclude. In retrospect "law's century" has been the practitioners' century. In the professional law school of the 20th century theories successively have faded out. Legal science turned out to be a professional craftsmanship. Laura Kalman has described the ignorance and arrogance of the American legal profession towards the academia. First with the Critical Legal Studies (CLS) legal science in new forms was brought back to the American law school. During the post-war period in Germany the judges of the Third Reich infiltrating the post-war judiciary were defined as "terrible jurists" (Furchtbare Juristen) who continuously adjusted to the ruling political system.[45]

This survey has demonstrated the different legal contexts between the countries we have studied. In Germany the law faculties since the early modern times had cooperated with the judiciary through *Aktenversendung, i.e.* [that is] sending the minutes in a case from the court to the faculty of law asking for advice or a decision. This regular interaction between practice and theory was discontinued with the new national procedural laws in 1877. In the U.S. the theoretically oriented Langdell law school was wide apart from the legal education which the young lawyer got as a practitioner when he rode the circuit. Langdell and Harvard Law School introduced the alternative. And in

---

[44] A.O. Winroth, Rättsväsende och juridisk utbildning, Stockholm 1906.

[45] Ingo Müller, Furchtbare Juristen. Die unbewältigte Vergangenheit unserer Justiz, Kindler Verlag: München, 1987; Bernd Rüthers, Entartetes Recht. Rechtslehren und Kronjuristen im Dritten Reich, 2nd ed., C.H.Beck: München 1989.

Sweden the legal education traditionally was aimed for a career as civil servant. So it was in the 17th century and so it still was around 1900. In 1906 the Swedish Bar Association, founded in 1887, was a small and relatively unimportant private organization. The Swedish Bar didn't play any role regarding the legal educational reform. This was a case in which only state institutions had jurisdiction.

The main problem in the modernization of the legal education was how the law professors should identify themselves as teachers: Were they educating future members of the university or members to be of the Bar and judiciary? That problem created more or less schizophrenic law professors and amazed practitioners. Most of the law professors—like Alfred Ossian Winroth—fought for their ideal concept: A balance between Theory *and* Practice. The law professors of the early 20th century aggressively fought for more practice, but from the view of the legal scientists this was a Pyrrhic victory. In reality they were on the defence. The consequence of the orientation towards practice also meant that the faculty of law successively insulated itself from the other parts of the university. The professional schools were not any longer real parts of the university. The law professors of the 19th century in some sense still were polymaths. They were included in the scientific work of the theologians, historians and philosophers. In 1906 there were still professors in penal law and in private law in Lund, who had started their professional careers as legal historians. At Uppsala most of the legal historians of the 20th century have been recruited from the history department.

The concept of legal modernity, with strong state legislation, welfare state economy and the social realities as contexts surrounding the legal science eroded successively the historical and philosophical instruments, which the law professors so intensively had used during the 19th century. Instead sociology became the modern field of the 20th century. Roman law as well as legal history, however, faded out, and back of the theoretical tradition of the 19th century remained only a living ruin, which we, the law professors of the early 21st century, still try to keep alive.

John Henry Schlegel

On a Possible Instance of the Transmigration of Souls: From American Regal Legalism to American Legal Realism and Back Again

When it comes to American legal theory and American legal education there are two parallel stories that, as Leonard Cohen would say, "Everybody knows." With respect to legal theory the story goes something like this. First, there was the "formative period," a time of the optimistic creation of an American common law, if you believe Roscoe Pound, or a time of capitalist transformation of the common law, if you believe Morton Horwitz. The Formative period was followed by a period of high formalism, a deadening calcification of the common law that reflected a refusal to deal with the industrial economy that developed after the Civil War. Then came American Legal Realism, a movement that overthrew formalism, and, after either a brief return to formalism called legal process theory, or a necessary correction of the excesses of realism called legal process theory, take your pick, brought forth the great cornucopia of legal theory that we have today. The reader may insert a list ranging from constitutional strict construction to queer theory and select appropriate adjectives of approbation or disapprobation, as you see fit, but recognize that we are all Realists now.

The story of American legal education is remarkably parallel, though with significantly different valences. Corresponding to the formative period, there is the period of apprenticeship, during which a few law schools bravely struggled on, but the bar as a whole lost control of the profession. Corresponding to the formalist period, there is the period of the rise of the Harvard Law School, the slow spread of the case method through out the land, the increase in previously abysmal educational standards for admission to the bar and the professionalization of law teaching. With Realism came the recognition that teaching law as a formal set of logically justified rules was a terrible idea, that the old categories needed to be replaced by a more functional approach and that law students needed to be taught that they were policy makers. After the unfortunate interregnum/necessary correction, take your pick, of legal process theory, came the great expansion of the law schools, their welcoming/not welcoming enough, again, take your pick, of women and people of color into the ranks of first students and then teachers, the growth of clinics, and the great fracturing of law that has created the kaleidoscopic curriculum of today, only Law and Butterflies and Garlic and the Law have yet to be offered—which together again shows that we are all Realists now.

So much for what everybody knows. For me, both of these stories might be examples of the concept of the transmigration of souls, also known as metempsychosis or reincarnation, for what they assert is that the spirit of the law, as made manifest in the form of legal theory or legal education, has inhabited successive bodies, successive understandings of what law was properly understood to be. Of course, both narratives could be read equally well, and indeed are regularly read, as stories of the law's progress. The shift from formalism to contemporary legal theory and from apprenticeship to the contemporary law school is endlessly portrayed as the climb from more primitive to more sophisticated understandings of law and legal institutions. One, but only one, of the reasons why I wish to suggest that these stories might be examples of the transmigration of souls is to eliminate that progressive, teleological valence from them, for transmigration assumes that the new body that a soul inhabits may be of the same kind or even a lesser kind of being. Thus, for the time being, I wish to call into question just what these well-known changes may add up to, whether it is true that "We are all Realists now." Doing so requires that I describe what I mean by Realism, a dangerous thing, as well as a complicated one, but here goes.

Brian Leiter's most important insight into law is his observation that American Legal Realism can best be understood as a species of literary naturalism. When Llewellyn urged that scholars "See it fresh, see it new," he might have been invoking the literary realism of first Balzac and George Eliot, and later John Galsworthy, Henry James and Edith Wharton. But, when he added to this a reference to the social sciences, he had shifted his focus to the naturalism of Zola, Theodore Dreiser, Jack London, and Frank Norris. The shift in understanding, and thus objective, that is suggested by this progression of authors, is from a concern with accurately reproducing immediate experience, the common actions of individuals that illuminate their character and the consequences of those actions, to a concern for the social determinants or scientific laws that underlie or control these actions and consequences. This is a switch from individual psychology to Holmes' "man of the future, the man of statistics and economics," to sociology or economics or anthropology or perhaps group psychology, but in any case a shift toward a social scientific understanding of law.

Realism embodies this shift, but still makes sense only as a response to formalism, and vice versa. Formalism is, however, easier to describe than Realism, so let me digress for a moment. Formalism is the proposition that law is a discipline; the historic legal formalists would have used the word "science" meaning a rational ordering that is self-contained, whereas the more recent word is "autonomous", in that its propositions are understood to be logically interrelated in such a way that no knowledge, not to be found within the system, is needed to formulate a proposition that is part of the system.

This is that American Regal Legalism that I spoke of in my title. My title, and this understanding of formalism, draws on first, "Regal," a sense of the increasingly "imperial" nature of the American economy in these years, and second on "Legalism," Judith Shklar's still useful book with that title. Shklar writes that legalism is "the ethical attitude that holds moral conduct to be a matter of rule following, and moral relationships to consist of duties and rights determined by rules." For her, "its most nearly complete expression is in the great legal systems of the European world." In this world, which I believe is the American world as well, she says, the urge to draw a clear line between law and non-law has led to the constructing of ever more refined and rigid systems of formal definitions. This procedure has served to isolate law completely from the social context within which it exists. Law is endowed with its own discrete, integral history, its own 'science,' and it own values, which are treated as a single block sealed off from general social history, from general social theory, from politics and from morality.

In a shorthand way of putting it, the rules of law are all one has to know in order to do or understand law. American Legal Realism denies that this is the case. It asserts that to understand and/or do law, one needs to know things other than the rules of law, though exactly what one needs to know is left conspicuously unspecified. But, among other things, somehow doing law realistically, and so being a Realist, requires knowledge of the social sciences seen as empirical disciplines. Realism supported its denial that law is—and here comes a weasel word, "properly" understood as formalism, by denying that formalism was a science. The claim that the Realists made was that the only proper sciences were empirical, that formalism for all of its claim to be scientific was not empirical, as evidenced by the fact that it understood that the objects of its study, that is, the cases, could be wrongly decided and so discarded in ways that physical facts could not be discarded when attempting to explain them. For Realists it was thus obvious that theory was trumping fact and so formalism's pretension to be a science, bogus.

Not wholly surprisingly, Realism made this claim in a way that it saw as scientific, as empirical, but empirical in two different senses, as can be seen in the following table.

A Modest Typology of Legal Realist Research in Law and Legal Institutions

	Library Research	*Field Research*
Better Law	Cook on Conflict of Laws Green on Torts	Clark: Civil & Criminal Cases Douglas on Bankruptcy
	(Corbin on Contracts)	
	Hutchins on Evidence	"The Johns Hopkins Boys" on Civil and Criminal Cases
		Marshall on Petroleum
	Llewellyn on Commercial Law?	
Better Understanding of Legal Institutions		
	Arnold on Anti-Trust	Moore on Banking Moore on Parking and Traffic
	Frank on Judicial Decision-Making	
	Robinson on Legal Institutions	

In the sense that is most easily understandable to contemporary lawyers, law professors and law students, the Realists asserted that a researcher needed to go out in the world, out into the field, and examine how law was working in existing legal institutions. Thus, Charles E. Clark and his associates at Yale, and Leon Marshall, Herman Oliphant, Hessell Yntema and their associates at Johns Hopkins, looked at how civil and criminal cases moved through both state and federal courts. Clark and others looked at the compensation provided to victims of auto accidents. William O. Douglas looked at the cases that moved through bankruptcy courts. And, J. Howard Marshall, lately of Anna Nichole Smith fame, studied petroleum regulation. However, there was another sense of "empirical" that the Realists understood, one that is less familiar to us, though we engage it more often. They believed that it was possible to be empirical in the law library, and in two ways. First, some Realists took seriously the formalist's claim of science and looked at what the courts were doing, rather than what they were saying. This is what Walter Wheeler Cook did in the area of the conflict of laws and by Leon Green in torts. Such work provides the basis for the claim made by William Twining and others that Arthur Corbin was a Realist, "a case law realist." Second, other Realists would scour the library for the results of other social science work, generally at the level of the theory that was derived from someone else's field research, and apply those theoretically informed research results to assertedly known legal phenomena. This is what Robert Maynard Hutchins and his associates did in the area of evidence law. Karl Llewellyn's work on the roots of sales law in nineteenth century commercial practices also might be included, though as often, his work resists classification.

These two kinds of Realist empiricism—field and library—would be easy to understand, were that all that Realism produced. Unfortunately, this scholarship, rooted in the Progressive era, in the Poundian tradition of concern for generating better, or better understood rules of law, was only one aspect of empirical scholarship by the Realists. There was an entirely different kind of empiricism practiced by the Realists in both the field and in the library. This scholarship focused on gaining better understanding of legal institutions, primarily the courts, especially in judicial decision-making, but also law, seen more generally as a process involving lawyers, courts, legislatures, the executive and administrative agencies. Such work seemed unrelated to the progressive search for the better law or even better institutions. Field research of this kind is exemplified by the work of Underhill Moore, who tried to find out whether it was true that law followed custom and who also attempted to see how effective legal sanctions were by looking at the regulation of parking. In the library the most famous work was that of Jerome Frank who used Freudian psychology to understand judicial decision-making. Thurman Arnold also used theories about symbolic behavior to understand business regulation in general, and anti-trust law in particular, and Arnold's colleague, Edward S. Robinson, used a mixture of sociology and psychology to examine legal procedure generally. Karl Llewellyn's work on the roots of sales law in nineteenth century commercial practices instead might be included here.

So, the Realists attacked formalism with a two by two table. One might think of this as something rather odd. But it is not really. One needs to remember that the Realists were all liberal law professors. In one way they were just trying to do a better job of teaching law. In another, they were liberals in a very conservative time.

Progressivism had died out in World War I and in the aftermath of that war the country turned rightward, as the presidential terms of Harding, Coolidge and then Hoover, made modestly clear. Progressive reformers had talked a great deal about trying to understand how the law worked, but had done very little to actualize the seemingly empirical program implicit in their claim. Liberal law professors seemed to wish to strive both to be better academics, that is, teach better and do better scholarship, and be of service to society and to be effective liberals.

These humans remembered the catch phrase from the days of the old Progressives, "the law on the books and the law in action." They, who like most of us, see no reason why better teaching and better politics are not the same thing, could and did read this phrase two ways. One was that the job of the law professor was to work to change the law on the books and the law in action, so that they were one and the same, so that there was a better law. On this reading, the task of field and library research was to produce the facts that would cause all men of good will to act so as to bring the adoption of that better law. The other was that the job of the law professor was to understand how and why the law on the books and the law in action were different. On this reading, the task of field and library research was simply that of gaining an understanding of the institutions of law. Such an understanding might lead toward creating better institutions, but might also lead simply to working more effectively within the existing institutions. One seemed to be a shade more directly political; the other, a shade more academic. Yet, both implied the need for a more thoroughly empirical approach to law, picking up where the Progressive lawyers had dropped the ball.

It was the former reading of the task of law professorial scholarship, of bringing about better law, that Pound and other progressives wanted law professors to do. Some of the Realists, such as Cook, Green, Hutchins and perhaps Llewellyn, Clark, Douglas, Marshall and "the Hopkins boys", worked in their own ways to do just that. But the other reading of the task of law professorial scholarship, of developing better understanding of legal institutions, was available to law professors as well, at least to those who wondered why the progressive tradition had died out. One might simply try to understand why, no matter what one did, the gap remained, for such a concern led directly into work trying to understand the institutions of law. Some of the Realists—Frank, Arnold, Douglas, Moore and perhaps Llewellyn worked in their own ways to do that, too. All saw, but in different ways, the need for a more thoroughly empirical basis for their separate work.

In practice, however, because formalism was a court-centered understanding of law and because the progressive legal project had been focused on judicial objection to legislative actions altering common law principles, our memory of Realist scholarship is less focused on work on the substance of legislative or judicial law-making, much less on the nature of legal institutions, than on the process of judicial decision-making, on but one square, the lower left one, in my two by two table. Here is where the great contemporary debates about Realism occurred. And here the Realists offered three critiques, the logical, the psychological and the sociological, that have come down to us today.

The logical critique argued that legal concepts were not a constraining force to law. For this critique, Realists relied on the work of Wesley N. Hohfeld, an analytic philosopher and anything but a Realist, who argued that legal concepts inappropriately treated as unitary, a number of various discrete legal relationships, any one of which could not be implied from the existence of another. Realists also relied on the work of Judge Benjamin N. Cardozo, who asserted that there were four methods for deciding a case, and so the judge was allowed the "sovereign prerogative of choice" between them; and on the work of Cook, who claimed that legal rules "hunt in pairs," so that for every rule there is an exception or counter rule whose application would lead to a different result; and finally on the work of Llewellyn who identified a great range of acceptable techniques of dealing with a precedent. Together these observations suggested that legal concepts did not produce results by logic alone, but rather permitted judges a choice of results, a choice that was made surreptitiously, as it were, without explicitly considering the function that the rules played in society or the policy behind those rules.

Similarly, the psychological critique argued that judicial opinions, traditionally presented in a seemingly syllogistic form, hid the real sources of decisions. For this critique, Realists relied on the work of Judge Joseph Hutchinson, who argued that most cases were decided on the basis of a "hunch" about the appropriate result, and on the work of Frank who argued that a judicial opinion was but a rationalization of a decision reached otherwise, so that formalism was motivated by an infantile search for paternal authority and that a truly adult judge would recognize and expose the many factors, particularly the idiosyncrasies of his response to the facts proven at trial, that lead to the choice made in an individual case. These observations suggested that judges obscured the real factors that operated in particular cases behind a web of false necessity.

The sociological critique attempted to identify the factors at work behind the facade of the judicial opinion. Here, the most common arguments made by Realists drew on the work of William F. Ogburn, who posited that social understandings of the world commonly lagged behind the practices that these understandings purported to describe. Versions of this concept of "cultural lag" were offered to explain how it was that judges utilized an "outdated" economic theory to understand labor conditions or commercial transactions, or an "outdated" psychological theory to understand witness testimony, or an "outdated" political theory to limit governmental regulation of economic activity. It was only here that the Realists' jurisprudence, as that word is traditionally used, met up with their interest in empirical research directed to yielding better law. Faced with the facts gathered from such research, it was assumed that judges and other legal actors, as men of good will, would come to abandon their outdated theories.

The Realists relied on their sociological critique to draw together their attacks on formalism by positing that the major problem with law was the lack of a relationship between concepts and categories of the law and the "realities" of modern life. Closer attention to these realities would allow one to focus law's attention on institutions, including the courts, but equally importantly on such activities such as organizations of businessmen in a trade association, and on the functions these institutions performed. Such an analysis would disclose when the law needed updating because of its lag behind social practice, and would also expose circumstances where the law was dysfunctional, that is, where a body of doctrine was ineffective, as, for example, when Arnold argued that the anti-trust laws provided the comfort of a myth that law was doing something to address public fears about big business, while ignoring the anti-competitive practices that made for effective monopoly power. Such exposure might then force law to develop effective and appropriate social policy for the conditions of modern life.

Conceivably, both approaches to the legacy of Progressivism, namely, the focus on better law and the focus on a better understanding of legal institutions, could fit not just into the law professor's scholarship, but also into the classroom. Focusing on the law in action meant that one might continue the formalist project of justifying the law on the books through criticism, and yet shift from justification based on logical entailment, which was the only possible way a formalist could justify, other than by an unquestioning positivism, the success or failure of law to do what it was supposed to do, to achieve what we today, its policy goals. In the alternative, focusing on understanding law might help young lawyers understand their jobs once they were out in practice and might even allow them to conceive of ways of effectively bringing about that better law, either because the lawyer knew how judicial decisions were really made or what brought forth favorable legislative or administrative action.

Understanding how law worked might be a lever for liberal politics in a conservative time and could make for more effective liberal policies when that time passed.

However, both of these were approaches to teaching, easy to dream about, easy to focus on when not paying too close attention to that relative of the mantra about law in the books and the law in action, namely, the difference between what is taught and what is learned. However, when it came to actually incorporating the results of the Realists' empirical research into the daily grist of classroom discussion it was less easy to be dreamy. The person who had to report on efforts in that direction, Charlie Clark in his role as producer of decanal annual reports, started out quite optimistic. "Teaching in the School should ... be richer and more worthwhile as materials are collected." Within a year he was lamenting that "one of our problems is to bring this body of material into the ordinary day-to-day bounds of the student." And when it came to his creating his own casebook on Civil Procedure, Clark, not a modest man, mentioned his own empirical research but once, and that briefly. A second edition doubled his references to this work.

A few odd scraps of Realist writing and practice related directly to legal education need to be noted before looking at what Realism has contributed to current legal education, examining in detail the evidence for the transmigration of souls. First, though there was much talk of shifting to more functional categories for organizing legal education, little of this took place. Most of it can be seen as name changing. Thus, the course in Persons turned into the course in Domestic Relations and the separate courses in Agency, Partnership and Corporations got packaged together as the law of Business Associations. Second, and more important, was the introduction of courses in Labor Law, Federal Taxation, Anti-Trust and Administrative Law, all recognizing the growing federal legislative activity that was pushing its way into what was once seen as an education focused on the study of common law. Third was the singular claim of Frank that the law schools ought to focus more on clinical education, such as the medical schools offered to its third and fourth year students. Last was the modest opening-up of the casebook form. In his constitutional law casebook Thayer had pioneered the addition of notes to the books of unedited cases that Langdell had created, largely as a way of limiting the wear and tear on the reporters in the Harvard Law Library. The Realists built on this practice by adding certain "non-legal" materials, such as excerpts from non-law books, and such things as contracts or legislative provisions to their casebooks. This was said to be a big deal.

From what I have said so far, it ought to be reasonably apparent that Realism was more than just a series of writings about jurisprudence, as well as why those writings bulk so large in our memory of the movement. It was just very hard to do what Clark, Douglas, Marshall and "the Hopkins boys" did out in the field. Indeed, Clark eventually became a Federal judge, Douglas quickly grew tired of the work and became a Federal bureaucrat and Marshall became a very wealthy oilman. Oliphant, one of "the Hopkins boys", followed a similar pattern. The rest never tried any empirical legal research again. And, compared to their work, Moore's was unimaginably difficult, as basic research in any field is these days. Indeed, without the panoply of graduate students and post-doctoral assistants and loads of federal dollars that supports such research in the sciences it is almost impossible. Thus, most of the empirical research in law is now done by the various social scientists who dominate the Law and Society Association. All that may survive in the law schools of the Realist's program of empirical research is the library research.

So, it is time to begin to confront a question of the transmigration of souls. Are we all Realists now, so that the law and legal education is in some significant way different than it was in Langdell's day? Or has the spirit of formalist legalism, of American Regal Legalism, somehow come to inform an outwardly different law and legal education, that only appears to have been changed by

Realism? To address this question it is best to start with scholarship, for it is scholarship that most obviously distinguished Realism from what had come before.

The great success of policy analysis as a format for scholarship and teaching is surely Realism's greatest triumph. This should never be forgotten; logical entailment is largely dead except in certain obscure backwaters, where constitutional law meets liberty and property, for example. And most everywhere such an analytic framework is to be found, it acts just as it did in the Supreme Court the late nineteenth and early twentieth centuries . . . as an excuse for not confronting unpleasant changes on the part of a dominant social/economic class that feels itself under siege by the forces of unreason. However, if one looks at what passes for scholarship in these hard times, at what the commercial lawyers call merchantable goods, goods that pass without objection in the trade, one sees something that is, at the least, troubling.

Emboldened by the success of Frank and Arnold in importing theory from other disciplines into legal analysis, the contemporary law review article starts with its chosen problem, wait, no, that really isn't right; it starts with a theory, - law and economics, public choice theory, liberal rights theory, critical legal theory, feminist theory, critical race theory, queer theory, or what have you - then fits a problem to that theory. Thereby finding, to no one's surprise, that the theory fits the problem well, the article then asserts, much as would a law professor one hundred years ago, that the theory requires that the chosen problem be solved in one and only one way. As a result of this scholarship the reader learns nothing about the world, the objective of empirical inquiry, other than what the theory in question would prescribe as the solution to the chosen problem, a bit of learning that is surely obvious from knowing the theory.

This activity is in no sense an epistemic naturalism. Indeed, the tie to any empirical understanding of the problem in question is limited to a modest search on the internet designed to show that the problem in question is not so singular as to be trivial; a few cites to, or if length is important, a few reviews of the work of, others who regularly use the theory; and a bit of armchair understanding of what the facts must be. The tie to the world is surely thinner than was the case in Muller v. Oregon. What we have here is an example of the ancient and honorable legal form—the brief, unfortunately directed to no court in particular, offered on behalf of only an imaginary client, and likely to persuade only those who share the theory in question. It is what Pierre Schlag calls "normative legal theory", the assertion that a given normative framework compels a specific doctrinal result.

There is nothing "Realist" about the activity of producing normative legal theory. Not only does such work lack a meaningful tie to any possible empiricism, but more important it is structured as if all of the insights about judicial decision-making, for which the Realists are well known, are untrue. Indeed, it implicitly rejects all of the insights of the individual Realists whose work, based as it was on theory from other disciplines, made possible contemporary policy analysis, for it assumes that legal arguments are efficacious in and of themselves, that it does not matter "what the judge had for breakfast" or that the legal system is trying hard to assuage some peoples fears, but not do anything, to offer only the crudest understandings of the work of Frank and Arnold and Robinson, much less that of Llewellyn.

Indeed, such scholarship is not even an example of Cook or Corbin's case law realism. At least these men attempted to figure out why the cases came out as they did, what might have been the reason why otherwise intelligent people, whatever they might have said in fact, did what they did. In contrast, contemporary scholarship takes judicial words at face value, except to the extent that the relevant theory suggests that anyone not speaking in its language is hiding an antagonism to the results ordained by that theory. At best we have a gussied-up version of the dispute "whether the acceptance of an offer is effective when put in the mailbox or only when it is received", argued as it was for years without any understanding of the history of the English Postal Service. This does not sound like we are all Realists now.

Nor are we all Realists now in another sense as well. My friend Fred Hart, hearing that I was offering these remarks, hazarded that, from the perspective of one educated at Georgetown in the early Fifties, a time when Realism hadn't made its way to that school, Realism had made teaching doctrine very much harder. How this is might be the case is simple. Realism meant that there were no "right" answers. Perhaps there were better or worse ones, but even acting on Pound's assertion that a proper legal decision required that one balance the interests that the parties were taken to represent was a damn hard thing to do. Taken seriously, the answers one was able to come up with were almost all indeterminate, a result that students hated. And if not taken seriously, the activity easily degenerated into a bizarre, poker-inspired formalism: "ok, I'll call your freedom of contract, and raise you an unequal bargaining power!" Realism meant hard work in the classroom, reduced coverage and restless troops, not a nice package.

At the same time, Fred recognized that Realism made it easier to talk about institutions in the law school classroom. Unfortunately, almost no one in law schools knows much about any important institution that touches law except perhaps litigation, and that is a dying art form, except where for odd reasons we have decided to use the courts largely as an administrative bureaucracy. So, a discussion with a group of students about an institution that is part of doing law quickly degenerates into either a case of the halt leading the blind, and so the reification of uninformed prejudices, or into a lecture summarizing the literature. Either is deeply boring. As a result, the troops are even more restless than with long discussions of indeterminate policy analysis because an understanding of institutions won't be on the exam or won't be on the bar exam or worse, won't be on both.

If one looks away from scholarship and teaching to the minor topics that defined Realism, one immediately concludes that two topics have had no impact on legal education at all. No serious work has gone into reorganizing the categories of legal thought and it is unlikely that any will in the foreseeable future. Langdell might not recognize the category system of today, but Charlie Clark would. Similarly, the opening up of the casebook form has pretty much ground to a halt. Occasionally books based on problems appear, but most of these problems are simply hypotheticals designed to walk people through the relevant legal doctrine. The most that can be said for changes in the casebook form is that cases are now edited to within an inch of their life in an effort to cram more doctrinal details into the 800 page format.

It is possible that Realism midwifed the great proliferation of new and ever narrower courses that fill every respectable law school's curriculum. Still, it is not clear that any of the Realists would have welcomed such a development. While they did experiment with the seminar form, they stuck pretty closely to the old categories for the big courses. As for clinics, a development that only Frank advocated and only Llewellyn supported, and then only without credit, it is interesting that most of the existing clinics follow the model of poor people's law that Llewellyn advanced, but with the credit that Frank expected. Part of the problem is, of course, the bar. Most lawyers object to law students helping to do for free what they could charge for, something that Tom Lehrer sang about In My Hometown. But part of the problem is that most people attracted to clinical teaching and the faculty who wish to salve their political consciences by supporting clinical work, would find it unclean to offer a clinic devoted to money law - corporate transactions, commercial real estate, commercial bankruptcy or capitalist regulatory problems. Frank's clinical lawyer school has only been tried at the City University of New York, and there it has not flourished, but only hung on, even though it has since taken on the form of the simulation.

Could this state of affairs be otherwise? Might Realism be more of an influence on legal education today? I suppose so, though I have my doubts. Consider my teaching of late. First, I teach a contracts class where the materials are organized to follow the structure of the modern commercial contract. My students do two written assignments that force them to deal with such documents. Class time and exam time are given over to trying to understand how judges make decisions in contract cases. Next I teach in an introductory corporate finance course that is taught exclusively from documents used in a real transaction. The only textual materials are the web site of power point slides used by my management school colleague who teaches how to read financial reports and estimate entity valuation. The point of the course is to understand what transactional lawyers do and how they craft documents to help clients make the most out of their deals. Then there is a little course for corporate finance students surveying the legal specialties that support transactional practice. I call the course "Toxic Waste" because the point is to make clear to students that these other people do very complicated stuff and that skimping on their services by doing it your self is like playing with PCBs. Practitioners come in to explain what they do, and grades are based on memos, written to explain what aspects of the base transaction, that we work with in the course, suggest that a specialist's services would be necessary. This is a form of issue spotting, but in a world where the answers are expected to come from someone else.

Next year (2008) I will participate in a course that looks seriously at various institutional practices that explain the roles of varying financial players in transactions and the structure of the actual, on the ground markets in which deals are done, of markets ruled by imperfect competition, information asymmetries and humans with memories. This course will require students to use the descriptive theory built in class to produce a public presentation about an institution or market that has not been studied in class. And I participate in a full semester program that we offer in New York City were students get to study, then meet and talk with individuals who do money law of various kinds.

Now all of this is Realism with a vengeance. How do students respond? I know that most of my first year students hate the contracts course, because there are no rules that give answers and because they cannot imagine that figuring out how judges decide cases is part of a litigation practice. They don't want Realism; they want to do the trump card-word magic that they associate with law. The same is true for about half of the students in the introductory corporate finance course, who really can't understand how anyone could possibly work with so many variables, all of which put a practitioner's ass on the line. They too want law, by which they mean rules, not judgment. The students who continue on into Toxic Waste love the course; they have decided that they can deal with the chaos and are pleased to know that there really are some things that they don't have to understand completely. A few find that one of these ancillary practices is more suited to their taste and are thankful that we have shown them what they were. The students in institutions and markets will be almost uniformly unhappy that we have cranked up the level of analysis; some will see that these matters have been there from the beginning; in a dry run of part of this course offered this semester, one even thanked us for taking up a previously unacknowledged problem.

It is not fun dealing with all of these unhappy people. I endure their enmity by reminding myself that by steering them away from doing what I teach, I cut down on drug and alcohol abusing lawyers, if only modestly. At the same time, I love dealing with the other five people who teach in the area, as almost all of these courses are co-taught because no two of us share the same skills and knowledge base. Occasionally I am worried about the self-indulgence my love represents.

My kind of teaching is clearly not for anywhere near all of my colleagues. Most think that the corporate finance folks are weird; some, that we are dangerous. Springing this far free from the professional identity of the law professor as an explicator of doctrine through policy analysis is not attractive. Our theory is not the normative theory that they are comfortable with, that they associate with being a law professor, but the descriptive theory that is part of literary and epistemic naturalism. However, I do think that something like this work is implied by Realism.

As for my scholarship, I have published only two doctrinal articles in my life. One, a law review comment, followed its analysis with a prediction of how the Supreme Court would rule that I derived by counting noses, a choice that almost got me kicked off the Review. The other has a normative conclusion so weak that it seems to be, and was, an afterthought. While I have published some history, and continue to do so on occasion, most of my publications are either in the form of the review essay or are occasional poetry, such as this piece. Of late, I have even dropped pretensions and begun labeling pieces as pure essays, drawing on the French sense of that word, "to try," to attempt to think out a problem "in the area of law" that one hopes others may find interesting or helpful. So, I never speak as if I were, like the Pythia at Delphi, the oracle of the law.

Many of my colleagues are as bewildered by my scholarship as by my teaching. They are always polite at faculty seminars. Some are helpful. But on the rare occasions I take such work "on the road," to "legal theory workshops" as they say, I am greeted less hospitably. One prominent law professor refused to engage with a really rather good piece of mine, because when he asked whether I was "serious or merely having fun" in the piece, I hazarded that I was doing both. Others find my work quite odd. They want to know what legal change or remedy I would propose, and are unhappy when I say that I have no normative prescriptions, but that I am just trying to help people understand law. Again, I do think that something like this work is implied by Realism.

So, if I am right about my teaching and scholarship, it is doubtful that, "we are all Realists now." Rather, as usual, a lot of people know a lot of things that "just ain't so". Given the relentless normative focus to the way that we teach and write these days, our substitution of justification by normative policy analysis for justification by logical entailment, the stuff that we call teaching and scholarship, is anything but Realist. Realism didn't slay the dragon of formalism, and whatever Realism did for/to legal theory and legal education, and here again you may take your pick, as a result of this substitution, it seems that the matter of the transmigration of souls is properly at issue.

The substitution of one form of legalism, one separation of law from, in Shklar's words, "the social context within which it exists," so that it is "sealed off from general social history, from general social theory, from politics and from morality," for another, is not obviously anything more than the substitution of one body for another. American Regal Legalism is alive and well, indeed I believe that, unfortunately, it is the soul of American law, transmigrated to today. I think that Realism, with its focus on two varieties of empirical research, might be seen to have tried to escape legalism. That it failed ought to give us pause as we discuss legal education in comparative and cultural perspectives. Before we conclude that great things are, or even might be, happening, we might consider why a previously heralded transformation came to so little, while seemingly "everybody knows" that it accomplished so much.

Bruce P. Smith*

Legal Education in the Twentieth Century: Continuity, Change, Convergence?

Prompted by the chapters in this volume, this contribution seeks to address three questions. First, how influential were the pedagogical initiatives undertaken by Gleason Archer at the Suffolk Law School in the early decades of the twentieth century? Second, how enduring were the contributions of the Legal Realists – particularly, with respect to empirical legal studies? And, finally, should we anticipate convergence in the characteristics of law schools across the globe in the years to come? Put differently, will law schools – whether in Boston, Berkeley, Berlin, Buenos Aires or Beijing – increasingly share a common pedagogy, research orientation, organization, and mission or are they likely to continue to exhibit important institutional variations?

I. Gleason Archer and Practice-Oriented Pedagogy

As Robert Gordon has observed, the history of U.S. legal education since the late nineteenth century has demonstrated a curious distance between classroom pedagogy and actual practice. By 1900, the practicing bar – at least in major urban centers on the East Coast – had largely turned its attention to "local law," including state corporation law and municipal regulations. Despite these developments, leading law schools continued to teach common-law subjects, unmoored to the laws of any particular state or municipality and, thus, seemingly indifferent to the needs of workaday lawyers. And while urban law firms continued to grow, and the demands on lawyers continued to increase,

* Dean and Guy Raymond Jones Faculty Scholar, University of Illinois College of Law. This chapter expands upon comments offered at a conference on Globalization & the U.S. Law School: Comparative and Cultural Perspectives held at the Suffolk Law School in Boston on January 25-26, 2007. I am grateful to Stephen Hicks for his kind invitation to participate and to the Suffolk University Archives for access to their rich collection.

"no school with pretensions altered its basic approach in the face of the changing character of law practice."[1]

Not all legal educators, of course, believed in the arid abstractions of the case method or the divorce between legal education and legal practice. In his *Introduction to the Study of Law in Suffolk Law School*, published in 1919, the founder of Suffolk Law School, Gleason Archer, candidly asserted that he "[did] not believe in the case system, so-called, as a method of teaching." Instead, Archer's Suffolk curriculum covered state-law subjects – such as the statutes of Massachusetts – and exposed students to "problems" designed to simulate real-life issues.[2] Other urban law schools catering to working-class students also disavowed the case method in favor of practical instruction. Beginning in 1908, The Detroit College of Law required its students to attend proceedings in the city's courts and to brief, plead, and argue cases in the College's own "Justice Court," "Circuit Court," and "Supreme Court."[3]

Although this practice-oriented pedagogy was out of step with early twentieth-century Langdellian case method, it notably does not jar the sensibilities today. To the contrary, Archer's themes have a peculiarly modern ring. Writing in 1910, he observed acidly that "[t]he law graduate of today finds himself strong in theory of law, but nearly as ignorant of how to practice law as when he entered ... law school."[4] In recent years, similar cries have been heard among judges, hiring partners, legal educators, and even the very accreditation bodies and foundations that caused Archer's Suffolk Law School so much grief. On the latter score, both the American Bar Association (ABA) and the Carnegie Foundation have called for law schools to adopt more practical skills-based courses.[5] Moreover, there have been increasingly vocal pleas that law schools teach state-law subjects, including state constitutional law, on the ground that a law school curriculum focused purely on national

---

1 Robert W. Gordon, Legal Thought and Legal Practice in the Age of American Enterprise, 1870-1920, in Professions and Professional Ideologies in America (Gerald L. Geison ed. 1983), reprinted in John H. Langbein, Renée Lettow Lerner, and Bruce P. Smith, History of the Common Law: The Development of Anglo-American Legal Institutions 967 (2009) [hereinafter History of the Common Law].

2 Gleason L. Archer, Introduction to the Study of Law in Suffolk Law School (1919).

3 Gwenn Bashara Samuel, The First Hundred Years are the Hardest: A Centennial History of the Detroit College of Law 41 (1992).

4 Gleason Archer, Law Office and Court Procedure vii (1910).

5 See ABA Standard 302 (requiring skills-based training) and Carnegie Foundation for the Advancement of Teaching, Educating Lawyers: Preparation for the Profession of Law, Summary, 5-6 (2007) (noting that the case method "consists in the abstraction of the legally relevant aspects of situations and persons from their everyday contexts" and calling for greater skills-based learning).

topics does not adequately prepare students to practice.[6] In these respects, Archer's commitment to practice-oriented pedagogy and state law looks prescient, not peculiar.

II. Legal Realism and Empirical Legal Studies

If aspects of early twentieth-century legal pedagogy appear to have been resuscitated in recent times, so, too, have approaches to legal research – no more so than in the realm of empirical legal study. In this regard, there is perhaps greater continuity between modern-day legal scholarship and the Realist enterprise than Professor Schlegel allows.

In his *American Legal Realism and Empirical Social Science*, Professor Schlegel has convincingly demonstrated how American legal realists, in the 1930s, turned to social science and empirical legal study as a means of criticizing legal formalism.[7] According to Professor Schlegel, the Realists' empirical enterprise bore disappointingly little fruit. There is no doubt that several factors made it difficult for 1930s-era Legal Realists to sustain the momentum behind their empirical projects: the organizational and interpersonal challenges of interdisciplinary collaboration; the difficulty of reaching agreement on acceptable social science norms; the equivocal nature of the Realists' findings – what Bob Gordon has described, in their worst modes, as "a piling up of data without any theory to structure them";[8] and the crushing economic burden of the Depression, which made it difficult for scholars to secure adequate funding for costly empirical work.

Despite these challenges, several of which remain today, empirical legal studies have actually fared extremely well on U.S. law faculties over the past decade. In recent years, the field has spawned its own publication – the *Journal of Empirical Legal Studies*. Conferences devoted to the subject have become increasingly common.[9] At my own law school, we offer a team-taught course

---

6 In recent years, the plea has been made most passionately by The Honorable Jeffrey Sutton of the U.S. Court of Appeals for the Sixth Circuit. See Jeffrey S. Sutton, Why Teach – and Why Study – State Constitutional Law, 34 Okla. City U. L. Rev. 165 (2009). I am grateful to Judge Sutton for bringing this article to my attention.

7 John Henry Schlegel, American Legal Realism and Empirical Social Science (1995).

8 Robert W. Gordon, Professors and Policymakers: Yale Law School Faculty in the New Deal and After, in History of the Yale Law School: The Tercentennial Lectures x (ed. Anthony T. Kronman, 2004) [hereafter Yale History].

9 Indeed, on the day before this article went to press, I received a flyer announcing an Inaugural Colloquium on Empirical Legal Studies to be held at the Cornell. Subjects to be addressed include empirical studies of employment discrimination, settlement, and damages.

on Empirical Legal Methods using a casebook recently published by three of our faculty members.[10] And other colleagues on my faculty have published empirical studies of civil litigation and insurance law, a quantitative analysis of the disposition of patent cases, and an ongoing empirical study of consumer bankruptcy filings.[11]

These projects would certainly be recognized as "empirical" by Legal Realists like William O. Douglas (who himself engaged in massive empirical studies of business failure), by scholars of administration (like Charles Clark), by the institutional economist and realist Walton Hamilton (who wrote monographs entitled "Milk," "Whiskey," and "The Automobile Tire"), or by the legal realists at Columbia and Yale who undertook studies of tort compensation in automobile accidents. To be sure, twenty-first century empiricists have moved from the study of milk, whiskey, and tires to civil litigation, intellectual property, and bankruptcy. Few adopt the methods of an Underhill Moore, who chronicled traffic patterns in New Haven, Connecticut, while his wife delivered food to his intrepid student-observers. [12] But empirical legal study – in short, the capacity and willingness to *count* things – remains very much alive.

III. Institutional Convergence or Divergence?

The previous discussion has suggested that legal education has exhibited certain important continuities across points in time with respect to pedagogical approach and research methods. Can similar continuities be found across nations? When Boston-based legal scholars travel to Sweden or Swedish-based legal educators venture to Boston, do the worlds they encounter increasingly look alike? Are we, in short, moving to a point where legal education will be globalized and universal, and where our approaches to teaching, research, organization, and mission will have converged?

There is certainly plentiful evidence of cross-border influence. Recent reforms in legal education in the Far East have brought law schools in Japan

---

10 Robert M. Lawless, Jennifer K. Robbennolt, and Thomas S. Ulen, Empirical Methods in Law (2010).

11 See David Hyman, Do Defendants Pay What Juries Award?: Post-Verdict Haircuts in Texas Medical Malpractice Cases, 1988-2003, 4 J. Empirical Leg. Stud. 3 (2007) (with Bernard Black, Kathy Zeiler and Charles Silver); Jay P. Kesan & Gwendolyn G. Ball, How are Patent Cases Resolved? An Empirical Examination of the Adjudication and Settlement of Patent Disputes, 84 Wash. U. L. Rev. 237 (2006); and Robert W. Lawless & Elizabeth Warren, The Myth of the Disappearing Business Bankruptcy, 93 Cal. L. Rev. 745 (2005).

12 See generally Schlegel, American Legal Realism, supra note 7.

and Korea closer to the U.S. model.[13] For their part, émigré legal scholars have exerted great influence in the United States, England, Israel, and other nations.[14]

But as with the fate of legal transplants more generally,[15] the fate of cross-border initiatives in legal education is contingent and uncertain. As Professor Reimann notes, continental émigré scholars made relatively little impact on U.S. legal scholarship – at least compared with their prodigious talents. And this state of affairs prevailed despite the fact that American legal thinkers had been looking to the Continent for over a century. In the early decades of the nineteenth century, American legal writers had familiarized themselves with the writings of German jurisprudes.[16] Harvard's Charles Eliot was prompted in the late-1860s to reform both his University and his law school based on his travels to a number of German academic centers, including Heidelberg, Marburg, Stuttgart, and Tübingen.[17] Reimann's own work has pointed to the influence, albeit refracted, of German legal thinkers on Justice Oliver Wendell Holmes.[18] And as both Professor Reimann and Modeer have observed, the German "free law" movement, in its effort to account for how judges elect to address the uncomfortable "gaps" in codified law, influenced twentieth-century American Legal Realists.[19]

U.S.-born legal developments have also encountered challenges abroad – no more so than in the case of the law and economics movement. By most accounts, the turn towards economic analysis of law has been the most influential development in U.S. legal scholarship in the last generation. [20] Yet

---

[13] See, for example, Tom Ginsburg, Transforming Legal Education in Japan and Korea, 22 *Penn State International Law Review* 433 (2004).

[14] John H. Langbein, The Influence of the German Émigrés on American Law: The Curious Case of Civil and Criminal Procedure, in Der Einfluss deutscher Emigranten auf die Rechtsentwicklung in den USA und in Deutschland (ed. Marcus Lutter, Ernst C. Stiefel & Michael Hoeflich, 1993); Mirjan Damaška, A Continental Lawyer in an American Law School: Trials and Tribulations of Adjustment, 116 U. Pa. L. Rev. 1336 (1968); Mathias Reimann, Stepping Out of the European Shadow: Why Comparative Law in the United States Must Develop Its Own Agenda, 46 Am. J. Comp. Law 637 (1998); and Jurists Uprooted: German-Speaking Émigré Lawyers in Twentieth Century Britain (ed. Jack Beatson & Reinhard Zimmermann 2004).

[15] See Alan Watson, Legal Transplants: An Approach to Comparative Law (2d ed. 1993).

[16] Michael Hoeflich, Translation and the Reception of Foreign Law in Antebellum America, 50 Am. J. Comp. L. 753 (2003).

[17] David S. Clark, Tracing the Roots of American Legal Education: A Nineteenth-Century German Connection, 51 Rabels Zeitschrift für ausländisches und internationals Privatrecht 313 (1987).

[18] Mathias W. Reimann, The Common Law and German Legal Science, in The Legacy of Oliver Wendell Holmes (ed. Robert W. Gordon 1992).

[19] See also James Herget & Stephen Wallace, The German Free Law Movement as the Source of American Legal Realism, 73 Va. L. Rev. 339 (1987).

[20] See, classically, Richard A. Posner, Economic Analysis of Law (1973).

the influence of the movement in Europe has been considerably less dramatic. Although a seminar in Law and Economics occurred, precociously, at the University of Lund as early as 1974, there remained ”no regular law and economics seminars at any Swedish university” by the late-1990s. In short, law and economics in Sweden simply failed ”to become an integral part of legal research.”[21]

Given the successful colonization by the law and economics movement of U.S. law faculties, what explains the failure of the movement to take hold in Sweden? One hypothesis is that public law schools in Sweden may have been reluctant to appoint scholars whose free market orientation might have been at odds with the central tenets of social democracy. Another possibility is that applied economics had a lowly stature in economics faculties, including in Sweden.[22] Whatever the reason, it is important to note that some educational transplants – even ones capable of growing aggressively in some climates – do not take well in different places.

Moreover, even when species of legal thought do flourish across borders, they are likely to adapt and evolve in different ways, in response to local conditions. Consider, in this regard, the intellectual movement known as Scandinavian Legal Realism, closely associated with the writings of Axel Hägerström (1868–1939), the noted philosopher at the University of Uppsala in the early decades of the twentieth century. Generalizing broadly, the Scandinavian Legal Realists expressed deep suspicion of natural rights, claiming that fundamental legal conceptions like ownership were ”maintained by magic” rather than ”grounded in observable and testable reality.” In this manner, they shared certain conceptions with American Legal Realists, including the distrust of legal maxims and the importance of ”observable ... reality”.[23]

But there is a reason why we continue to speak of ”American” Legal Realism and ”Scandinavian” Legal Realism – and I don't think that the reason is simply to indicate geographic source. Rather, the movements continue to be understood as intellectually distinct in important ways. American legal realists

---

21 Göran Skogh, Law and Economics in Sweden, in Encyclopedia of Law and Economics, available at http://encyclo.findlaw.com/0390book.pdf.

22 Id.

23 See Gregory S. Alexander, Comparing the Two Legal Realisms – American and Scandinavian, 50 Am. J. Comp. L. 131 (2000) and Michael Martin, Scandinavian and American Legal Realism (1997).

drew upon psychology (in the case of Frank), anthropology (in the case of Llewellyn), and institutional economics (in the case of Hamilton). By contrast, the motivating spark for Scandinavian Realism resided in the realm of philosophy, and these and other differences (including the nature of the reformers' respective missions) represented important differences that cannot be easily papered over.

All of this is simply to suggest that legal education – even in an increasingly globalized age – is likely to exhibit important contingencies and cultural variations across borders. This suggests that, while attempted transplantations may well occur at an even more rapid pace in the years to come, considerable national differences will likely remain. In my judgment, we should not lament if certain transplants do not take hold or if diversity continues to characterize the legal-educational landscape. To the contrary, we should celebrate such an outcome. As ecologists are prone to note, there are benefits to diversity. An ecosystem whose flora or fauna are weighted too much towards one species may be susceptible to disease or destruction. To make the point in legal terms, jurisdictional variation encourages healthy innovation and healthy competition.[24]

Conclusion

Writing in 1910, Gleason Archer observed that "[t]he law is so vast in its scope that ... [a] lawyer cannot hope to *know* all the law on a given point, but he may reasonably hope, by careful investigation, to *find* the law on that point in his or in other jurisdictions."[25] Like the lawyer, the legal historian suffers from the impossibility of knowing all that he or she might wish to know.[26]

The history of legal education, like other fields of legal history, has suffered from these gaps in knowledge. But it has also suffered from what Anthony Kronman, the former Dean of the Yale Law School, has called an "unattractive species of congratulation" – the tendency to celebrate rather than critique.[27] In a brilliant review essay published a generation ago in the *Harvard Law Review*, Professors Schlegel and Konefsky incisively observed that the then-

---

[24] See, for example, Larry Ribstein & Erin O'Hara, The Law Market (2009).

[25] Archer, supra note 4, at viii.

[26] Regarding this theme, see, most famously, F.W. Maitland, Why the History of English Law is Not Written (1888).

[27] Yale History, supra note 8.

existing institutional histories of law schools tended to share a common narrative trajectory:

> Simply put, the school grows from humble, but auspicious, beginnings to early triumphs and then through occasional hard times, though with never more than a momentary temptation to backslide from fixed and noble goals, to a place – if only a small place – in the sun.[28]

A generation later, as exhibited by the contributions to this volume, scholars of legal education have increasingly cast aside this standard mode of "law school history" and adopted a more comprehensive, more chronologically expansive, more comparative, and more critical mode of analysis. And in this, happily, there is still much to celebrate.

[28] Alfred S. Konefsky & John Henry Schlegel, Mirror, Mirror on the Wall: Histories of American Law Schools, 95 Harv. L. Rev. 833, 836 (1982). Indeed, the history of the Suffolk University Law School arguably exhibits a similar narrative arc: a humble but heroic beginning in a Roxbury parlor; early challenges with finances, local rivals, and accreditation bodies; and, in time, a triumphant centennial celebrated in a state-of-the-art building. For details regarding Suffolk's early history, see Michael Rustad, *The Impact of History on Contemporary Prestige Images of Boston's Law Schools,* 24 Suffolk L. Rev. 621 (1990) and History of the Common Law, supra note 1, at 970-74.

Mathias W. Reimann*

We are all Globalists now – The Heritage of the Émigré Jurists for American Legal Education in the Second Half of the Twentieth Century**

In the second half of the twentieth century, American legal academia has been influenced by a steady stream of émigré jurists[1], the most widely noted contingent being the refugees from the Nazi regime who arrived mainly in the 1940s. There is now a substantial and impressive body of literature about the role they played in the United States (as well as in England)[2]. Yet, the coverage of this literature is limited in two important regards. First, it addresses only the émigrés' biographies and scholarship; it by and large does not discuss their impact on legal education, i.e., on teaching and the curriculum. Second, it focuses only on the refugee generation; it says nothing about its successors, i.e., the émigrés who arrived from the 1950s onward.

This essay discusses the contribution of the émigré jurists to American legal

* Hessel E. Yntema Professor of Law, University of Michigan; Dr. iur. utr., University of Freiburg 1982; LL.M., University of Michigan 1983. I am indebted to several scholars for contributing their own memories and impressions to this essay: Richard Buxbaum, William Fisch, Mary Ann Glendon, Jim Maxeiner, Ugo Mattei, and especially to Eric Stein who is the last survivor of the first generation of émigré jurists.

** This paper is a slightly reworked version of a talk given at the Suffolk Law School's conference on the occasion of its 100th anniversary in Boston, Mass., January 26, 2007.

1 By "émigré jurists" I mean legal scholars who came to the United States already as lawyers, i.e., after having received at least their basic legal education in continental Europe. Thus, I do not count among them immigrants who arrived in the United States at an earlier age and first studied law in an American law school (or other common law country), such as Thomas Buergenthal, Richard Buxbaum, John Fleming, or Oliver Lissitzyn.

2 See especially Marcus Lutter, Ernst C. Stiefel & Michael Hoeflich (eds.), Der Einfluß deutscher Emigranten auf die Rechtsentwicklung in den USA und in Deutschland (1993); Ernst C. Stiefel & Frank Mecklenburg, Deutsche Juristen im amerikanischen Exil (1933–1950) (1991). For England, see Jack Beatson & Reinhard Zimmermann, Jurists Uprooted (2004). The broader story of the exodus of European scholars to the United States is told by Laura Fermi, Illustrious Immigrants (1968) (on legal scholars see especially 352–353). A more narrowly focused study of emigré influence on American law is Jutta Klapisch, Der Einfluß der deutschen und österreichischen Emigranten auf contracts of adhesion und bargaining in good faith im US-amerikanischen Recht (1991).

education roughly from World War II to the turn of the twenty-first century. It focuses primarily on those who came from Europe because the requisite background information about them is easily available and because what expertise I have is limited to that group. This focus is also adequate because on the whole, the Europeans have comprised the largest, as well as most the influential, group of legal scholars coming to the United States in the second half of the last century. Still, we must not forget that since World War II, jurists from other parts of the world have also entered American legal academia, enriching it in various ways[3]; the assessment of their contributions would have to be the topic of another paper.

I will begin by looking at how the first generation of émigrés came into the country and provide some numbers and names (infra. I.). We can then assess their impact on legal education in the United States and will find that the subjects they and their immediate successors shaped (or at least helped to shape) by and large lingered on the margin of the curriculum for several decades (II.). Yet, when we move forward to the 1990s and beyond, we will see a grand awakening to the émigrés' agenda in the form of the current efforts to "globalize" American legal education (III.). This leads us, finally, to ask how much credit for the current developments goes to the émigré jurists (IV.)

I. Coming into the Country[4]: Numbers and Names

The most well-known, as well as the largest, group of émigré scholars consisted of refugees from Nazism who fled Germany, Austria, and, to a lesser extent, other areas occupied by Germany in the 1930s and 1940s. Most had to leave because they were Jewish, others on account of their political views. In 1933, about 1200 academics were immediately dismissed by the Nazi-regime from German universities alone, and the number of ousted scholars rose steeply over the next couple of years. Many, but not nearly all, emigrated. By 1939, about 2200 scholars of all disciplines had left Germany[5]. Often, they first went

---

[3] A major example of the (now) older generation is Boris Kozolchyk who came to the United States from Cuba and has for many years served as the Director of the National Law Center for Inter-American Trade at the University of Arizona. Another person in that group is Ved Nanda who immigrated from India and has become an authority in various areas of international and comparative law.

[4] The title is borrowed from John McPhee, Coming into the Country (1977), a well-known book about Alaska.

[5] These data are taken from Jack Beatson, Aliens, Enemy Aliens, and Friendly Enemy Aliens. Britain as a Home for Emigré and Refugee Lawyers, in Beatson & Zimmermann, supra note 2, 73, 87.

to another European country, especially to England, from where many then continued to other parts of the world. Over a quarter, and perhaps as much as a third, of all émigré scholars eventually came to the United States—hundreds all in all[6].

As far as legal academics in particular are concerned, one source gives the number of those immediately dismissed as 132 and maintains that 69 eventually left their fatherland[7]. We know of about three dozen legal scholars who finally arrived in the United States[8]. All these figures should be considered approximations.

Among those who managed to establish themselves as legal academics in the United States, more than a dozen became widely known. Most of them found appointments in leading, or at least highly respectable, law schools: Edgar Bodenheimer (UC Davis), Carl Fulda (Texas), Albert Ehrenzweig (UC Berkeley), Wolfgang Friedman (Columbia), Friedrich Kessler (Yale), Herbert Kronstein (Georgetown), Kurt Nadelman (Harvard), Arthur Nussbaum (Columbia), Max Rheinstein (Chicago), Ernst Rabel (Michigan), Stefan Riesenfeld (Berkeley), Rudolf Schlesinger (Cornell), Louis Sohn (Harvard), Eric Stein (Michigan), and Hans Zeisel (Chicago). Of course, such a list is somewhat arbitrary because there were others who might also be included, depending on the criteria one employs: Hans Kelsen whose appointment, however, was in Berkeley's political science department[9], not at Boalt Hall; Hans Morgenthau, again, ultimately not a legal scholar but an international relations specialist at the University of Chicago[10]; David Daube, who, however, came to the United States only in 1970[11], and several perhaps less familiar names like Brigitte Bodenheimer, Eberhard Bruck, Adolf Berger, Adolf Homburger, Arthur Lenhoff, and Ernst Levy. Even that list is not complete in any sense.

What did these scholars do, and what was their impact on American legal education?

---

[6] See id., at 84; Stiefel & Mecklenburg, supra note 2, 41.

[7] Beatson, supra note 2, at 87.

[8] See the list of short biographies in Stiefel & Mecklenburg, supra note 2, pp. 41–68. That list is almost certainly incomplete (and the number given in the text almost certainly too low) because it contains only those who met with some professional success in their new home. Others who could not establish themselves professionally in the United States left no easily traceable historical record.

[9] On Kelsen, see Clemens Jabloner, Hans Kelsen (1881–1973): Leben – Werk – Wirkung, in Lutter et al., supra note 3, at 521.

[10] On Morgenthau, see Stiefel & Mecklenburg, supra note 2, 105–107.

[11] On Daube, see Alan Watson, David Daube, in Lutter et al., supra note 2, 549.

II. The Impact on Legal Education: Lingering on the Margin

One can imagine two principal ways in which the émigré scholars could have influenced law teaching in the United States: first, by importing European teaching methods, and second, by affecting the curriculum.

1. Teaching Style: European Influence?

With regard to teaching-style, the émigrés' had something to offer that their indigenous American colleagues could not easily provide and that might have its attraction even in an American classroom: a systematic approach providing a general overview and elucidating the basic structures of the law. Mirjan Damaska, himself a (later) émigré scholar, aptly called this "a panoramic view" and the "grammar of law" [12].

The émigrés were used to a teaching method which differed sharply from the technique prevailing in American law schools at the time. In contrast to case analysis and Socratic method with their close attention to particular facts and their emphasis on inductive reasoning from case to rule, the continental European training consisted mainly of exposition in lecture form with an emphasis on the law's systematic coherence and on deductive reasoning from rule to case. Most of the émigrés had ample opportunity to bring such a more expository and systematic style into the American classroom. After all, they normally taught not only subjects with a foreign component but spent most of their time teaching courses on domestic American law. Some actually became leading scholars in their respective fields, such as Friedrich Kessler in contracts, Max Rheinstein in family law and decedents' estates, and Stefan Riesenfeld in bankruptcy.

It is not easy today to find out how they actually taught in the classroom because most of them are dead and because even the memories of their students, now themselves near or in retirement, have often faded. What I learned from those I asked suggests a very mixed picture[13]. Quite a few of the émigré scholars adopted the classic American teaching method of quizzing

---

[12] Mirjan Damaska, A Continental Lawyer in an American Law School: Trials and Tribulations of Adjustment, 116 University of Pennsylvania Law Review 1363, 1364 (1968).

[13] I conducted personal interviews with Eric Stein about his own teaching; about Max Rheinstein's teaching style with two of his former students, William Fisch and Mary Ann Glendon; about the teaching of Edgar Bodenheimer, David Daube, Albert Ehrenzweig, Carl Fulda, Friedrich Kessler, Stefan Riesenfeld with Richard Buxbaum; and about Rudolf Schlesinger also with Richard Buxbaum as well as with Ugo Mattei, James Maxeiner.

students in the Socratic style—Albert Ehrenzweig, Carl Fulda, Friedrich Kessler, Stefan Riesenfeld, Rudolf Schlesinger, and Eric Stein. Others, however, adhered to the lecture method, like David Daube. Some mixed the exposition of the material with asking questions, like Edgar Bodenheimer, and some emphasized problem solving, like Max Rheinstein. At least a few started out Socratically but over time resorted more and more to lecturing; Eric Stein and, apparently, also Rudolf Schlesinger are cases in point[14].

This mixed picture is not really surprising because one can think of forces pulling in both directions. On the one hand, Socratic teaching came somewhat naturally to those émigrés who had gone back to school in the United States and had thus become brainwashed in the American way. In many cases, it was also motivated by the émigrés' wish to adapt to their new environment, not only in order to survive professionally but also perhaps as a token of gratitude to their new academic homes[15]. At least in some instances, adopting the case method resulted from frustration with their own legal education in Europe (i.e., the boredom of many lectures) in contrast to which the American teaching style was more engaging and enjoyable[16]. On the other hand, old habits die hard and often reassert themselves after initial enthusiasm for new methods. Lecturing also allowed teachers to cover more material, and it resulted from the traditional European need to provide at least some coherence and some kind of a systematic overview.

On the whole, there is no evidence that the émigrés had a major influence on American teaching technique, in particular, that they influenced it in the

---

[14] Eric Stein said of himself that his teaching became less socratic over time as he found it more and more necessary to lay out the material in a more systematic fashion. Richard Buxbaum experienced a very socratically-minded younger Rudolf Schlesinger while Jim Maxeiner and Ugo Mattei, who were Schlesinger's students a generation later, reported that he was mostly lecturing.

[15] The latter reason has been suggested in a slightly different context by John Langbein, The Influence of the German Emigrés on American Law: The Curious Case of Civil and Criminal Procedure, in Lutter at al., supra note 2, 321, 330. This resonates with a conversation I had with Hans Zeisel at the University of Chicago in 1985.

[16] In addition, some of the émigrés, such as Wolfgang Friedman (see John Bell, Wolfgang Friedman, in Beatson & Zimmermann, supra note 2, 517, 522) were connected, in one way or another, with the sociological branch of German jurisprudence which had its roots in the teachings of Rudolf von Jhering, in the early twentieth century free school of law, in the jurisprudence of interests, and in the *Rechtstatsachenforschung*. These movements were rather close to, and had in fact exercised considerable influence on, modernist American legal thought, especially the sociological jurisprudence of Roscoe Pound and Benjamin Cardozo, and on legal realism; see James Herget & Stephen Wallace, The German Free Law Movement as the Source of American Legal Realism, 73 Virginia Law Review 399 (1987). This connection between modernist German and American legal thought was particularly visible in émigré scholars like Arthur Nussbaum and Albert Ehrenzweig. For the émigrés who were steeped in the modernist (German) tradition, the transition to the American post-realist academic environment was facilitated, of course. Understandably, they felt little inclination to lecture American students on grand theories and abstract principles.

direction of lectures, deductive reasoning, and systematic exposition. Even if there were a few who pushed in that direction, their numbers were too small[17], their efforts (if any) too dispersed, and their environments too path-dependent to be seriously affected. It is true, of course, that over the last fifty years, American law teaching has gradually moved away from hard-nosed Socratic dialogue and minute analysis of appellate decisions towards more lecturing and problem solving. Yet that that is hardly due to the émigrés. It simply reflects broader changes in American legal education: law teaching has focused increasingly on statutes and regulations, constitutional theory and legal process—all of which do not particularly invite classical Socratic quizzing but rather induces a variety of teaching styles. In all this, the émigrés' fit right in but they left no particular mark on American classroom teaching.

2. The Curriculum: Comparative Law and Other Subjects

The more interesting question from today's point of view is whether the émigrés managed to influence American legal education by affecting the curriculum, especially in areas lying beyond the domestic American orbit. After all, their fame derived mainly from their work in comparative law, private and public international law, and, to a lesser extent, Roman and European Community law[18]. If we survey these areas, however, we find that until recently, all of them remained at the margin of the curriculum, albeit for rather different reasons; the lack of émigré influence on American legal philosophy and jurisprudence is a somewhat separate topic.

a. Comparative Law

The émigrés' most widely noted accomplishment was to establish comparative law as an academic discipline in the United States[19]. To be sure, they neither started from scratch nor did they do it alone. There was a long indigenous comparative law tradition, beginning in the nineteenth century and extending

[17] Notably, even among those who managed to establish themselves in American law schools, not all émigrés obtained full-time teaching positions; instead, quite a few, like Ernst Rabel at Michigan or Kurt Nadelmann at Harvard, became research professors with little or no involvement in actual legal education.

[18] The same is true for England, see Beatson, supra note 2, at 107.

[19] Emigré jurists also helped to get *The American Journal of Comparative Law*, the principal scholarly journal in that field in the United States, off the ground. While it was founded by a group of American scholars under the leadership of Hessel Yntema at Michigan in 1952, it drew heavily on the contributions of the foreign-trained law professors. The first issue contained articles by Ernst Rabel, Max Rheinstein, Heinrich Kronstein, and Edgar Bodenheimer; see 1 American Journal of Comparative Law (1952).

all the way into the twentieth, tied to names like Joseph Story, Ernst Freund, John Henry Wigmore, Roscoe Pound, and Karl Llewellyn, not to mention the tradition in civil law oriented Louisiana. Even in the foundational era of the 1950s, several leaders in comparative law, such as Hessel Yntema, John P. Dawson, and Arthur von Mehren, were homegrown. Still, the first émigré generation played a crucial role in putting comparative law on the American law school map as an academic discipline in its own right and for good[20]. It was Rudolf Schlesinger at Cornell who, in 1950, published the first, and perennially leading, casebook in that area[21], providing standard classroom materials and boosting the teaching of comparative law. It was Max Rheinstein who made comparative and foreign law teaching a staple at Chicago throughout the 1950s and 1960s. It was Stefan Riesenfeld and Albert Ehrenzweig who established a strong comparative law tradition at Berkeley. It was Carl Fulda who brought comparative law to the University of Texas. The list goes on. None of this would have happened without the émigrés—simply because establishing comparative law teaching required solid expertise in at least one foreign legal system which the émigrés had and which all but a handful of their American colleagues lacked.

As a result of the émigrés' efforts, comparative law became generally accepted as a course in its own right and its teaching enjoyed a period of slow but steady growth in the 1950s through the 1980s[22]. Gradually, a new generation of teachers took over. Many among them were émigré jurists themselves who, however, had left their European homes not because they were forced to flee but because they were looking for greener pastures: Hans Baade, Herbert Bernstein, Mauro Cappelletti, Mirjan Damaska, Friedrich Juenger, Walter Weyrauch, A.N. Yiannopoulos, and others[23].

Yet, during the postwar decades, comparative law never became part of the

---

20 This has been widely acknowledged in the literature, of course. See, e.g., Friedrich Juenger, Rudolf B. Schlesinger, in Lutter at al., supra note 2, 255, at 257; Reinhard Zimmermann, review of Lutter et al. (supra note 2), 1995 Zeitschrift für Europäisches Privatrecht 697, 701.

21 Rudolf Schlesinger, Comparative Law (1950).

22 This is indicated, e.g., by the number of American law school faculty who identified themselves as teachers of comparative law. According to the AALS (Association of American Law Schools) Directories of the respective years, that number rose from 30 in 1949–50 to over 300 in 1980. These numbers must be discounted, however, by the generally rapid growth of the teaching body in US law schools during that period. The (institutional) membership in the *American Society of Comparative Law* grew from 13 law schools in 1952 to 20 in 1960, 31 in 1970, and 42 in 1980.

23 A special case is Vera Bolgar who fled communist Hungary in 1949 and who, as Hessel Yntema's assistant at Michigan, became instrumental in establishing *The American Journal of Comparative Law*, see Alfred Conard, Vera Bolgar 1913–2003, 52 American Journal of Comparative Law 5 (2004). Vera Bolgar, however, was primarily a scholar and an editor, not a teacher, and her influence on legal education was negligible.

curricular core. It continuously suffered from lack of prestige, scarce interest by other faculty and moderate or low enrollment by students. Comparatists consistently complained about their discipline's marginal existence despite all the wonderful things they claimed it had to offer. When Günther Frankenberg wrote that comparative lawyers suffered from a "Cinderella Complex", the term acquired wide currency in the United States[24]; and John H. Merryman, looking back at a long career in the field, tellingly spoke of the "loneliness of the comparative lawyer"[25].

Why did comparative law not become a truly great success story? There were three principal reasons for the discipline's marginal existence from the 1950s through the 1980s.

First, American parochialism—much lamented by generations of comparatists—played a significant role. As Mary Ann Glendon put it with regard to her teacher Max Rheinstein, "most of his American students simply did not yet feel the need to deal with the fact of interdependence in a shrinking world, much less to acknowledge that we might have something to learn from another country's legal system."[26] Such a viewpoint was neither surprising nor necessarily absurd. In the postwar decades, it was not obvious what the victor of World War II should have to learn from the vanquished nations of continental Europe, their centuries-long legal traditions notwithstanding. This was especially true for Germany, which was barely getting back on its feet, remained dependent on American military protection, and struggled with its divided existence. Nor was it obvious to most American scholars what they should learn from France which had to be liberated through blood, sweat, and tears by the common law nations, nor from Italy which remained mired in corruption. Other countries like Switzerland or Austria seemed simply too small and insignificant to matter. Wasn't it telltale evidence of American legal superiority that European students were beginning to flock to American law schools rather than vice versa? Hard as it may be to admit, the much-maligned American arrogance of that period vis-à-vis Europe was not entirely without foundation.

Second, the fault also lay with comparative law itself. As I have described elsewhere in greater detail, the émigré generation shaped the discipline in the United States largely according to its European tradition, and that tradition fit

---

[24] Günther Frankenberg, Critical Comparisons: Rethinking Comparative Law, 26 Harvard International Law Journal 411, 419 (1985).

[25] John H. Merryman, The Loneliness of the Comparative Lawyer (1999).

[26] Mary Ann Glendon, The Influence of Max Rheinstein on American Law, in Lutter et al., supra note 2, 171, 178.

the American environment rather poorly.[27] This was true in several regards. To begin with, many of the discipline's avowed goals and objectives failed to resonate with the average American law student. Comparative law often claimed to teach knowledge for its own sake, i.e., as a matter of general education[28]; but future American lawyers in a professional school were rarely interested in pure intellectual enlightenment—they wanted knowledge with obvious practical utility which comparative law rarely delivered[29]. Furthermore, the discipline promised to show the relativity of legal rules, in particular their contingency on historical, social, and economic factors; but in contrast to its much more positivist European counterpart, American post-realist legal education by and large already taught that lesson within the purely domestic curriculum. Comparative law also claimed to spur law reform by learning from other countries; but since American legislators and judges paid no serious attention to foreign law at all, there was virtually no hope of actually using comparative arguments in the legislative or judicial arenas. Finally, comparative law teaching largely focused on substantive areas which were of secondary interest in the United States at the time. It was, again as a result of its European heritage, obsessed with private law, especially contracts and torts. In the United States of the 1950s through the 1980s, these were about the farthest things from hot topics[30]. Public law was constantly on the rise, and the attention-getting issues came from constitutional law and fundamental rights, criminal procedure and privacy, racial and gender discrimination, with labor, environmental, and consumer law not far behind. In all these areas, the émigré's comparative law had virtually nothing to offer. To be sure, there were a few exceptions, and where the discipline dealt with areas in flux at the time, such as family law or criminal procedure, it enjoyed some attention[31]. Still, its mainstream seemed quaint if not outright antiquated.

---

[27] See Mathias Reimann, Stepping Out of the European Shadow: Why Comparative Law in the United States Must Develop Its Own Agenda, 46 American Journal of Comparative Law 637 (1998).

[28] See Konrad Zweigert and Hein Kötz, An Introduction to Comparative Law (T. Weir transl., 3d ed. 1998) 15–16.

[29] Rudolf Schlesinger understood this and geared his casebook (supra note 21) largely towards such knowledge (e.g., pleading and proof of foreign law in American courts) which probably explains much of its success.

[30] An exception was products liability but in this area, Europe was way behind the United States and thus had little, if anything, to teach until quite recently.

[31] See, e.g., Mary Ann Glendon, State, Law, and Family: Family Law in Transition in the United States and Western Europe (1977); Mary Ann Glendon, The Transformation of Family Law. State, Law, and Family in the United States and Western Europe (1989); Mary Ann Glendon, Abortion and Divorce in Western Law (1987); John Langbein, Comparative Criminal Procedure: Germany (1977).

Third, there was a systemic problem with comparative law teaching. In order meaningfully to compare, one must first know something about at least two legal systems. The three-year curriculum in American law schools, however, barely sufficed to learn the basics of domestic law. Thus, comparative studies would have made real sense after the three year J.D. program, i.e., in a graduate setting. This is what Max Rheinstein offered at Chicago. Yet, as he found out, there was little interest—and thus little enrollment (at least on the American side)—in such a program[32]. After four years of college, three years of law school understandably exhausted most students' appetite for learning as well as their financial resources. What they wanted after obtaining their basic law degree was practical experience and income, not knowledge about foreign law or comparative insights. This was not an irrational position. After all, the effort of mastering a foreign legal system even in part is usually out of proportion to its practical utility for all but a handful of graduate students hell-bent on an academic career. It did not help, of course, that serious comparative law studies required some proficiency in at least one foreign language (especially at a time when materials about foreign legal systems written in English were still relatively scarce) which most American law students lacked.

b. Private International Law

The émigré jurists' efforts did not fare much better in the second area to which they made major contributions, i.e., private international law, also known as conflict of laws. In the United States, this field actually had a strong internationalist and comparative tradition especially in the work of Joseph Story[33] but that tradition got lost in the first half of the twentieth century when the discipline increasingly focused solely on interstate cases and concomittantly neglected the international dimension.

In the postwar decades, several of the émigrés, both of the first and the second generation, from Ernst Rabel[34], Kurt Nadelman[35] and Albert

[32] See Wolfgang Freiherr von Marshall, Max Rheinstein, in Lutter et al. 333, 337; see also Glendon, supra note 2, 178–79.

[33] Joseph Story, Commentaries on the Conflict of Laws, Foreign and Domestic (1834).

[34] Rabel's contribution was entirely on the scholarly side, especially through his *magnum opus*, The Conflict of Laws: A Comparative Study (4 vols. 1945–58). Rabel did not teach regularly in the United States and thus had no direct influence of legal education.

[35] Kurt Nadelman, Conflict of Laws, International and Interstate (1972).

Ehrenzweig[36] to Friedrich Juenger[37] and Phaedon Kozyris[38], valiantly struggled to bring the comparative and international approach, to which they had been accustomed in Europe, back to life in the United States. They were even ably assisted by some of their indigenous American colleagues such as Arthur von Mehren and Peter Hay. Still, most of their efforts were ultimately in vain. In the 1950s through the 1970s, American conflicts law sunk ever deeper into parochialism. The majority of the casebooks published during that period were virtually devoid of anything but domestic American law.

In conflicts law, however, the problem was not the émigrés' approach to the discipline; instead it was purely a matter of bad timing. The period when the foreign-trained scholars tried to bring international and comparative perspectives into the curriculum, was exactly the period when American conflicts law underwent a violent methodological "revolution". It was the era when first scholars and then courts largely abandoned the traditional approach in favor of a confusing panoply of more modern, policy-oriented, and often half-baked techniques. Virtually all attention was absorbed by handling the resulting turmoil on the purely domestic level. This left neither time nor will in the average classroom to consider, on top of it all, what other countries were doing or what special problems international cases presented[39]. One can justly lament how frequently American conflicts scholars reinvented wheels that the European experience had long ago proven faulty and how much they could thus have learned by looking abroad. It is nonetheless understandable that their capacities were exhausted by what was going on at home. As a result, for most of the postwar decades, the comparative and international perspectives pushed by the émigré scholars were largely considered exotic luxuries for which there was really no time.

---

36 Albert Ehrenzweig & Erik Jayme, Private International Law, A Comparative Treatise of American International Conflicts Law (3 vols. 1967)

37 Friedrich Juenger, Choice of Law and Multistate Justice (1993, special edition 2005); Friedrich Juenger, Selected Essays on the Conflict of Laws (2001).

38 See, e.g., John Kozyris, Values and Methods in Choice of Law for Products Liability: A Comparative Comment on Statutory Solutions, 38 American Journal of Comparative Law 475 (1990); John Kozyris, Conflict of Laws for Corporate Shareholdings: Predicaments and Prospects, in: Law and Justice in a Multistate World, Essays in Honor of Arthur T. von Mehren (James Nafziger and Symeon Symeonides eds. 2002) 295.

39 German conflicts scholar Gerhard Kegel famously accused his American colleagues of "stewing in their own juices" ("Kochen im eigenen Saft"), Gerhard Kegel, Wandel auf dünnem Eis, in Friedrich Juenger (ed.), Zum Wandel des internationalen Privatrechts (1974) 35, 41.

c. Public International Law and European Union Law

The émigrés' impact on public international law is more difficult to assess. Here, we must distinguish several dimensions of the issue. To begin with, some of the émigrés had no *direct* impact on teaching public international law simply because they were not much involved with it; this is true for two of the giants of international (law) theory: Hans Kelsen and Hans Morgenthau because neither regularly taught the subject (at least not in a law school). But they, and others, had an *indirect* influence by changing the way how legal scholars thought about, or conceptualized, public international law and, consequently, how they presented it in the classroom[40]. Yet another form of influence comes in the form of developing new courses and teaching materials or of exercising a strong influence on colleagues and future scholars[41]; the most important case in point was Wolfgang Friedman at Columbia from the mid-1950s to his death in 1973[42].

Beyond all that, some émigrés had a more concrete impact by establishing new special areas that have since become standard topics. One such case was Louis Sohn (a refugee from Poland) at Harvard whose casebooks on the United Nations[43] put the study of this (then still young) organization on the curricular map where it lives on today in the form of courses on *International Organizations* or the like[44]. The perhaps more salient case is Eric Stein (who fled the Nazis from Czechoslovakia) at Michigan who virtually founded the study of European Community law in the 1950s and 1960s[45], i.e., before the Europeans themselves really discovered it as an academic subject in its own right[46].

[40] On Kelsen, see A Tribute to Hans Kelsen, 59 California Law Review 609 (1971). Morgenthau was one of the founders of the school of "classical realism" in international relations studies, see Hans Morgenthau, Politics Among Nations: The Struggle for Power and Peace (1948, 6th ed. 1985). He thus paved the way for international law approaches that responded to the realists, such as the New Haven School, international legal process, and others.

[41] Much of this activity in the 1950s and 1960s was funded by money from the Ford Foundation which boosted international legal studies at various elite law schools. When the money ran out, however, the interest waned and international law became more marginalized once again.

[42] See Bell, supra note 16, at 530.

[43] See Louis Sohn, Cases and Other Materials on World Law; The Interpretation and Application of The Charter of the United Nations and of the Constitutions of Other Agencies of the World Community (1950); Louis Sohn, Cases on United Nations Law (1956).

[44] See, for example, Frederick L. Kirgis, International Organizations in Their Legal Setting (2d ed. 1993).

[45] See, e.g., Eric Stein, Peter Hay and Michael Waelbroeck, European Community Law and Institutions in Perspective (1963).

[46] In a similar fashion, émigrés launched the study of European Community Law in England in the 1960s and 1970s, see Beatson, supra note 2, at 103.

Particularly in Stein's case, the timing was perfect because he established the teaching of a subject just as the subject gradually established itself. European Community law was also a good fit with the traditional method of American law teaching because, similar to US-American constitutional law, its initial growth occurred almost entirely through case-law expounding a fundamental text, i.e., the decisions by the European Court of Justice in Luxemburg. Almost from the beginning, European Community law grew from its roots in public international law (i.e., a treaty) into a subject in its own right, especially because of its emphasis on the emergence of a common market, its peculiar form of federalism, and because of its gradual constitutionalization.

Yet, in the immediate post-World War II decades, even international law and its subcategories counted as rather specialized subjects in all but a handful of law schools. These topics were of academic interest merely to a few students and had immediate professional relevance only for the occasional graduate entering the State Department or other government service. European Community Law was regarded as even more esoteric and thus taught pretty much only where an individual faculty member took a particular interest in the subject. Here as elsewhere, the émigrés' teaching was not at center stage in the universe of American legal education.

d. Roman Law

Of all the areas in which the émigré jurists played a role, easily the least successful in the American curriculum was Roman law. As Michael Hoeflich has shown[47], Roman law had actually occupied a significant position in nineteenth century American legal education, especially during the so-called "formative period" of American law[48]. In the twentieth century, however, it had experienced a sharp decline both in scholarship and teaching. By the time the émigré jurists arrived, it was all but obsolete. Some refugees taught an occasional Roman law course here or there, and in later years, Alan Watson was among the few who averted the subject's complete demise in the United States. Ultimately, however, the European émigrés, steeped though many of them were in the subject, had virtually no chance to give Roman law teaching in the United a second lease on life. Quite aside from the students' lack of training in Latin, there was simply no sufficient academic interest in, and no professional need for, studying this topic.

---

47 Michael Hoeflich, Roman Law & Civil Law and the Development of Anglo-American Jurisprudence in the Nineteenth Century (1997).
48 Roscoe Pound, The Formative Era of American Law (1938).

e. Legal Philosophy and Jurisprudence

Finally, one may suspect some émigré influence on American legal philosophy and jurisprudence. After all, given the theoretical bent of German law teaching with its emphasis on philosophical underpinnings, general principles, and fundamental ideas, many, if not most, émigré scholars must have been steeped in the tradition of German idealism. Yet, there are few signs that the émigrés became very active in that field at all[49]. Arguably, there were a few exceptions. Hans Kelsen's *Pure Theory of Law*, and especially his concept of a *Grundnorm*, eventually became quite well-known in the United States[50]; Edgar Bodenheimer wrote occasionally on jurisprudence; and Wolfgang Friedman had published a textbook in that field in England[51]. Still, on the whole, the émigré's influence on American legal philosophy and jurisprudence was small, if not negligible.

One can think of several reasons for that phenomenon. First, legal philosophy and jurisprudence were virtually inactive at the time of the original émigrés' arrival. In the United States (and in England), the subject began to come (back) to life only after the publication of H.L.A. Hart's *The Concept of Law* (1961). Despite Lon Fuller's *The Morality of Law* (1964), it gained real momentum only in the 1970s with John Rawls, *A Theory of Justice* (1971) and Ronald Dworkin, *Taking Rights Seriously* (1977)[52]. By that time, the first émigré generation was retiring or dead. Second, perhaps the émigrés realized that (mainly German) idealist legal theory would not take roots the pragmatist and post-realist American soil. In particular, it must have been doubtful whether continental legal philosophy with its interest in broad questions about the law's essence and about the role of the state would have resonated with the American legal mind with its focus on the much narrower issues of adjucation and judicial review. Finally, German legal theory was probably widely regarded (correctly or incorrectly) as tainted by the Nazi experience and thus not a popular subject in American law schools in the post-World War II period, and the émigrés may well have understood that, consciously or not.

---

49 The same was true for Great Britain, see Beatson, supra note 2, at 103.

50 Hans Kelsen, Reine Rechtslehre (1934); the book's second edition (1960) was translated into English as *Pure Theory of Law* 5 (Knight transl., 1973).

51 Wolfgang Friedman, Legal Theory (1st ed. 1944, 5th ed. 1966).

52 In 1971, the California Law Review still prefaced its issue in honor of Hans Kelsen by pointing out that "many American lawyers, judges, and law professors are not primarily knowledgeable or interested in legal philosophy," so that "the name of Hans Kelsen rarely invokes in them the almost blind adulation or almost bitter hostility that not infrequently characterize the responses to Kelsen's work by legal and political thinkers in most parts of the world." Dedication, 59 California Law Review 607 (1971).

III. The Grand Awakening: "Globalizing the Curriculum"

In summary, the émigrés' influence on American legal education in the post-World War II decades is hardly a story of a smashing success. Not only did they have no visible impact on the teaching-style, they also did not manage to affect the core curriculum. Instead, the topics they were commonly associated with all remained somewhere on the margin of the curriculum (comparative law, private and public international law, European Union law) if they did not fall off the edge altogether (like Roman law). In other words, for most of the second half of the twentieth century, American legal education remained, on the whole, soundly parochial.

Yet, if we move forward to the last twenty years, we see an entirely different picture. Gingerly in the late 1980s, more obviously in the 1990s, and undeniably in the 2000s, the American law school curriculum has experienced the stellar rise of international, foreign, and comparative law teaching. Suddenly, these areas have become the fastest growing sector in American legal education[53]. In the last decade, one AALS conference after another trumpeted the need for "globalizing" the curriculum. Law schools are competing with each other for the lead in that endeavor. They are even beginning to *require* the study of international or comparative perspectives under a variety of models—arguably the most significant curricular innovation in decades[54].

With the exception of Roman law, all the major areas propounded by the émigré jurists of the first and second generation have suddenly become hot topics. There is a plethora of foreign and comparative law teaching, involving no longer only continental Europe but other parts of the world as well,

---

[53] In the 1990s, the rise international and comparative law course offerings outpaced that in other areas by a factor of almost 2:1, see Deborah Jones Merritt and Jennifer Cihon, New Course Offerings in the Upper-Level Curriculum: Report of an AALS Survey, 47 J.Leg.Ed. 524 (1997), 537 (table 2). According to the study reported in this article, between 1994 and 1997 alone, 265 new international and comparative law courses were added in American law faculties, compared with 152 new offerings in business and commercial law as the second largest category. For an overview of the vast array of such courses, see the summary on p. 539. The number of law professors considering themselves teachers of comparative law, which had risen gradually form the 1950s through the 1970s (see supra note 22), suddenly almost tripled between 1980 and today (rising from ca. 200 in 1980 to over 600 in 2006–07). The number of institutional (i.e., law school) members in the American Society of Comparative Law rose from 42 in 1980 to over 100 today (reaching ca. 50 % of all AALS member schools). Since 1990, more than 150 new law journals specializing in international and comparative law were founded.

[54] See, e.g., Mathias Reimann, Making Transnational Law Mandatory: Requirements, Costs, Benefits, 23 Penn State International Law Review 787 (2005).

especially East Asia and Latin America[55]. International and comparative conflicts law has largely mutated into International (Civil) Litigation which has become a field in its own right as well as a staple in many American law schools[56]. Public international law has spread throughout the curriculum, diversifying into a host of subcategories ranging from international organizations to human rights and international criminal law, and European Union law has established itself as an important field and is being taught in virtually all first-tier law schools and much beyond that[57]. Finally, a number of courses straddling the public/private (international) law divide have become commonplace, such as transnational law, international arbitration, and trade[58].

As a result, the current—third—generation of émigré jurists suddenly enjoys a position of unprecedented significance in American law schools. This increasingly diverse and rapidly growing group[59] is gradually attaining a degree of prominence previously reserved for teachers of constitutional law and of law and economics. In addition to their own faculty, US law schools today need and regularly employ hordes of foreign visitors from all over the world to teach international, foreign, and comparative subjects. Even among indigenous American law professors, interest in these topics is spreading fast.

---

55 See Curtis Milhaupt, Mark Ramseyer & Mark West, The Japanese Legal System (2006); Angel Oquendo, Latin American Law (2006); Kenneth L. Port & Gerald McAlinn, Comparative Law. Law and the Legal Process in Japan (2d ed. 2003); Daniel Chow, The Legal System of the People's Republic of China (2003); see also Larry C. Backer, Comparative Corporate Law. United States, European Union and Japan (2002).

56 The last few years have spawned a plethora of casebooks in that field: Charles Baldwin, Ronald Brand, David Epstein & Michael Gordon, International Civil Dispute Resolution (2004); Gary Born & Peter Rutledge, International Civil Litigation in United States Courts (4th ed. 2007); Thomas Carbonneau, International Litigation and Arbitration (2005); Andreas Lowenfeld, International Litigation and Arbitration (2d ed. 2002); Ralph Steinhardt, International Civil Litigation (2002); Russel Weintraub, International Litigation and Arbitration (4th ed. 2003). A good indicator of a field's status as an established teaching subject is the existence of a "Nutshell", i.e. a short summary for students: George Bermann, Transnational Litigation (2003).

57 The leading casebook is George Bermann, Roger Goebel, William Davey & Eleanor Fox, European Union Law (2d ed. 2002). There is also, again, a "Nutshell" for students: Ralph Folsom, European Union Law (4th ed. 2004).

58 In England, comparative law teaching has also been on the rise in the last few decades, see J.A. Jolowicz, Comparative Law in Twentieth Century England, in Beatson & Zimmermann, supra note 2, 345, 362–364.

59 Many arrived, again, from Europe but an growing contingent now hails from other corners of the world, especially Israel, Latin America, and increasingly, Asia.

IV. A Belated Triumph? – The Legacy of the Émigré Generations

In a sense, the current globalization agenda in American legal education is the émigrés' belated triumph. For decades, the first and second generation had pushed to bring more comparative and international perspectives into American classrooms. Now, suddenly, the third generation is seeing it happen. Yet, how much credit for the current developments do the earlier émigrés deserve?

One answer is: not very much at all. The main reason for the current rise of comparative and international law in American legal education is not the influence of the émigrés but rather the post-cold war globalization craze that has gripped the country and, along with it, American legal educators as well as a large percentage of students. Suddenly, the insight is spreading like wildfire that American law is interconnected with all parts of the world as a result of the globalization of the economy, of communication, and of the mobility of at least the upper strata of society. After decades of more or less happy parochialism, there is virtual panic in many quarters not to miss the global boat. How much of this is an appropriate (though curiously belated) reaction to a changing world or rather a fashion feeding on itself is an issue that I will not try to resolve.

Another answer is that the émigré jurists deserve substantial credit for the current developments. This is not because without them, American legal education would remain parochial even today—it wouldn't because what is happening in the world would force it out of that habit anyway. But without the émigrés, American law teaching would have had to start its globalization business from scratch, rather than hitting the ground running. The émigrés of the post-World War II decades built several pads from which we can now launch our current agenda with amazing rapidity.

On the most general level, the émigrés created, and then kept alive, a modest but persistent tradition of looking beyond the domestic orbit. As John Langbein put it, "within the American legal academy the émigrés left us a collective legacy, a tradition of serious attention to foreign example both as a valuable technique of problem solving, and as a subject of profound intellectual fascination." [60]

More tangibly, they were instrumental in creating a body of literature on foreign, comparative, and, to a lesser extent, international law that has

[60] Langbein, supra note 15, at 332.

provided a foundation for teaching in these areas. Of course, they did not create this body single-handedly because much, if not most, of it came from American authors. Yet, whoever it was who ultimately put pen to paper, most of this literature is the result of the synergy between the two groups. Edgar Bodenheimer co-authored his *Introduction to the Anglo-American Legal System* with his American colleagues at Davis[61]; Rudolf Schlesinger's pathbreaking casebook ultimately turned into a cooperative enterprise[62]; and Mary Ann Glendon's competitor volume would not exist but for her studies under Max Rheinstein[63].

Equally important were the training and the inspiration the émigré jurists provided for future generations of comparative and private international law scholars in the United States. It is true that they never created schools of disciples in the (rather feudal) European manner. Yet, they did motivate many domestic, and quite a few foreign, law students to embark on careers of comparative and international law in the United States[64].

Perhaps most importantly, the émigrés built personal and institutional bridges across the Atlantic from which their successors and particularly the present generation have profited in myriad ways. They were instrumental in bringing hundreds of foreign graduate students to American law schools many of whom then obtained influential positions at home, and they created various exchange programs for both teachers and students. Especially those foreign visitors who eventually became law teachers themselves constituted an invaluable resource. They have returned as visiting professors, in turn invited their American colleagues to their respective countries, or even co-taught with them here and abroad. In short, if American law schools today have ties with legal scholars virtually all over the globe, they are benefiting in no small way from the connections often initiated by the earlier émigré generations.

Last, but not least, many of the émigrés played an important role in building or expanding the foreign and international components of more than one American law library. Without their expertise and foreign language skills, this

---

61 Edgar Bodenheimer, John Oakley and Jean Love, An Introduction to the Anglo-American Legal System (2d ed. 1988).

62 Rudolf Schlesinger, Hans Baade, Mirjan Damaska, and Peter Herzog, Comparative Law (5th ed. 1988).

63 Mary Ann Glendon, Michael Gordon and Christopher Osakwe, Comparative Legal Traditions (1985) was dedicated to Max Rheinstein.

64 Probably the most successful teacher in that regard was Max Rheinstein whose influence on future comparative law scholars was broad and pervasive; see Freiherr von Marshall, supra note 32, at 339. At least Mary Ann Glendon, John Langbein, Courtland Peterson, and William Fisch fall into that category.

expansion would either not have happened at all or at least would have been much less impressive. And without our substantial collections of foreign, comparative, and international (including European Community) materials, the current globalization of the curriculum would hardly be possible.

Still, the émigrés' legacy is not only an asset, it is also a liability. This is especially true in comparative law. The postwar generations shaped this field, and to some extent even the study of foreign and international law, in ways that can create serious problems for the teaching of these subjects today. As mentioned, the European-style comparative law established by the first émigré generation fit rather poorly into American classrooms to begin with. To make matters worse, its approach also became outdated over time. One reason is that it has focused entirely on national legal systems, while today, an increasing portion of law is made and applied on the international level—in the UN, EU, the WTO, NAFTA, etc.; this, in turn, requires an understanding of the relationship between international and domestic regimes. Also, the émigrés' (understandable) Eurocentrism has become a real obstacle at a time when other parts of the world have risen to power and prominence. In addition, the émigré generation was often obsessed with finding similarities and promoting legal unification; this attitude has become potentially dysfunctional as we face a growing need to learn how to manage difference and as we have come to value diversity. Finally, the European tradition of rigidly separating private and public law creates a barrier that is increasingly artificial and thus frequently more harmful than helpful in areas such as (international) conflicts law, European law, or trade regulation.

The current generation must therefore critically review the émigré jurists' heritage. It must discard what has become obsolete or dysfunctional, build on what remains useful, and develop its own ideas that fit current needs. Fortunately, that work has already begun[65]. None of this implies a lack of respect for our forebears, quite to the contrary. As Nietzsche once said: "You repay your teacher poorly if you remain forever his student."[66]

---

[65] See, for example, Symposium: New Approaches to Comparative Law, 1997 Utah Law Review 255 (1997); Symposium: New Directions in Comparative Law, 46 American Journal of Comparative Law 597 (1998); Pierre Legrand and Roderick Munday, Comparative Legal Studies: Traditions and Transitions (2003).

[66] "Man vergilt einem Lehrer schlecht, wenn man immer nur sein Schüler bleibt." Friedrich Nietzsche, Also Sprach Zarathustra (1883–1885), Kritische Gesamtausgabe vol. VI, 1, p. 97.

Thomas Lundmark

Legal Education in Germany

Legal education at German universities is unusual if not unique in its concentration on preparing students for the so-called first state examination, which is explained below. The two-year internship known as the *Refendariat* will also be described, as will the second state examination, which follows completion of the *Referendariat.*

Before describing the admission process at universities and legal education offered there, it might be useful for the reader to consider a list of themes that will appear in the following discussion. These themes, or "forces", were at work in motivating the recent reform of German legal education, and they are likely to crop up in future discussions.

One of the most important forces at work in Germany affecting the legal education is the Europeanization and globalisation of the law. Not only do Germans in all walks of life have more contact, for trade and other purposes, with European and other countries, but one also can discern a certain Europeanization of the law in many areas. In fact, European law is (still) taught as a separate course, implying that European law is separate and distinct from the national law ordinarily taught at German universities. But this is changing. European law has been incorporated into the domestic law of Germany in many areas, ranging from consumer protection to employment law. Globalisation of the law is seen most clearly in the area of international trade, but international public law has played, and will continue to play, an increasing role in German legal education.

There has been a marked increase in the non-German population of Germany in recent years. The largest ethnic group are the Turkish Germans, although there are also large contingents of other minorities. One other significant, but diffuse, group are those people of German ancestry whose families emigrated to Eastern Europe and Asia, particularly to the areas of the former Soviet Union, which collapsed in 1991. Since then, over 3 million so-called *Spätaussiedler* have immigrated to Germany and been granted German citizenship. Despite their German ancestry, many of these new citizens have

East European or even Asian names, and few of them have German as their mother tongue.

Until the early 1990s, the 2.6 million people of Turkish ancestry living in Germany were, along with millions of members of other minority groups, prevented from becoming German citizens simply because Turkey and most countries in Eastern Europe, Africa, and South America had no procedure for expatriation. For if an applicant for German citizenship could not prove that he or she had been expatriated by his former state, he could not be granted German citizenship. Due to this Catch-22, studying law was not particularly attractive for these non-citizen immigrants because much of the job market, including positions in the civil service, was closed to them. Amendment of the immigration laws caused a sudden increase in the number of non-German students who chose law as their major. At one university students of Turkish background make up almost a third of the law student population.

Because of a lack of state financial support, German law faculties, which until recently were all state-run, responded quite slowly to the digital revolution. Only recently have they obtained access to online commentaries and collections of legal periodicals and case law. Today all universities accord their students internet access, and all the legal faculties have access to data banks in German law over and above those that are not available for free over the internet. A number of universities, including Münster, grant students access to Westlaw and/or Lexis. The style of lecture is traditional. While many of the younger law professors use PowerPoint in their classes, most rely exclusively on overhead slides or upon the textbook (*Lehrbuch*) that they have often written themselves. Students do not prepare for class. Rather, they take copious notes and study from these notes, from the texts recommended by the professor, and from commercially available outlines, such as those offered by Alpmann Schmidt, the publisher of this guide.

The one privately run law school, the Bucerius Law School which is described in more detail below, has challenged German academic thinking about the content of the legal curriculum as well as about teaching methods. The state-centred, positivistic approach to law, with its strict interpretation of sources of law, is slowly giving way to a realisation that law in the globalized world is seldom codified. The 26,000 judges in Germany have been unable to handle the increase in litigation, with the result that far more cases than before are settled by the parties or in arbitration. In some jurisdictions "only" 30% of civil cases go through to trial, and this number is steadily decreasing as parties to international contracts decide to take their disputes directly to international arbitrators. Bucerius recognised this trend and designed its curriculum accordingly, offering courses in alternative dispute resolution, arbitration, etc. The traditional, state-run universities have been slow to act, owing in part to lack of state funding. Bucerius has also recognised that most of the negotiation and contracting on an international level in Europe is conducted in English, not German, and accordingly requires that students spend one term (see below) at an English-language law school. A number of state-run universities, including Münster, have instituted programs in foreign law taught in the foreign language (see below). These programs, though quite popular, are not mandatory.

Admission to the study of law

When they are about 10 years old, children in Germany who are considered college material, are transferred to a college preparatory school called a *Gymnasium* for the remainder of their schooling. In the past, pupils at the *Gymnasium* took their school-leaving examination (*Abitur*) at the age of 19, but this was recently reduced to 18 years of age. The percentage of school children referred to a *Gymnasium* differs widely by city and community, ranging from below 10% to over 50% in some communities. *Gymnasium* pupils take classes in German, Mathematics, Physics, Chemistry, Geography, Biology, Arts, Music, Physical Education, Religion, History, and Social Studies. They are also required to study at least two foreign languages, one of which is almost always English. Many grade schools also now have foreign language programs, usually in English, so that all graduates of a *Gymnasium* have a decent background in English, even if some of them have difficulty speaking the language. In the final year of *Gymnasium* students prepare to take the written and oral school-leaving exam, or *Abitur*, generally a prerequisite to the study of law at a university. The *Abitur* grade-point-average *(Durchschnittsnote)* consists of grades in various subject areas in which the pupil feels most confident. Some subjects, for example, History or German, are considered easier than others, such as Chemistry and Physics. In addition, the grading varies considerably throughout Germany. Grade inflation may account for the phenomenon that virtually no one fails the *Abitur*. The highest mark given is 1.0 and the lowest 4.0. Grades between 3.0 and 4.0 are considered quite poor. However, one should not lose sight of the fact that fewer than one quarter of the young people in Germany leave school with an *Abitur*, making holders of the *Abitur* a relatively select group. For 2005, 270,000 pupils earned the *Abitur* of which 21,000 chose law as their major at a university. The number of students choosing law has been declining in recent years.

Most males complete their compulsory military or civilian service directly following the *Abitur*. Although this compulsory service is referred to as compulsive *military* service, in fact a large majority opt to work as civilians in hospitals, schools, and the like. Because of this compulsory service, the young men who enter university are generally one year older than the women.

There are 45 universities at present in Germany offering full-time law courses preparatory to the first state examination. To apply one of these 45 public universities, a prospective student sends an application form with his or her *Abitur* GPA, place of residence, and list of preferred universities to a central agency. This agency mechanically assigns students to the first university on their list if that student has an *Abitur* GPA in the "one" category or lives near the university. Because the student who lives near a university is, with few exceptions, more or less automatically admitted to that university, German universities are all basically regional, drawing 90% of their students from the surrounding area. This fact goes a long way toward explaining why there are no Oxford, Cambridge, Harvard, or Yale universities in Germany. Nevertheless, certain state universities are more attractive than others and tend therefore to be more selective in the students that are referred to them. For example, while at some universities every student who applies is admitted, only about half of the students who apply to Münster are admitted.

In the mid 1970s the German Federal Constitutional Court, in a line of decisions reminiscent of *Brown* v *Board of Education* in the United States, decided that poor *Abitur* grades could not justify excluding applicants from a state university if the university still had classroom capacity for more students. Furthermore, the question of how much capacity the universities had was one reviewable by the administrative courts. As a result of these cases, students with very low *Abitur* GPAs are allowed to study at university. However, they are not admitted to study medicine and biology as the universities have been able to convince the courts that the teaching facilities in these fields of study cannot accommodate more students. The judges have stopped short of ordering the states to make more equipment and facilities available and, as a consequence, these two fields of study have what is known as a *Numerus Clausus*. One side effect of this judicial intervention into university education has been an unwillingness of university administrators to increase their teaching staffs for fear that they will be required to accept more students.

Another side effect is that state universities began competing for good students outside their regions.

To this point the discussion has only addressed the study of law as one's major at a university. In recent years it has become popular to study law as a minor with, for example, business or political science as a major. Ordinarily, as is the case in Münster, these students are taught in classes that are separate from the full-time law students, and the classes that they are taught are introductory in nature and not perceived as potential encroachments on the legal profession. That is not the case with the so-called *Wirtschaftsjurist* or "business lawyer". The *Wirtschaftsjurist* is a graduate of an institution of higher education called a *Fachhochschule*, which is similar to a polytechnic. A number of these *Fachhochschulen* (plural form) offer courses in business law for students who hope to find work as a business lawyer, but only as an employee, not a principal, as the degree does not qualify one for admission to practise as a *Rechtsanwalt* (attorney). Many *Wirtschaftsjuristen* (plural form) work as in-house counsel. There they draft contracts, negotiate deals, and advise their employer on day-to-day operations, including employment law. Some *Wirtschaftsjuristen*, along with graduates of administrative colleges, work for public agencies and in that capacity appear before court representing their agency even though they are not admitted to the practice of law.

The education of a *Wirtschaftsjurist* covers six semesters, or three years, and concludes with the granting of a degree of *Diplom-Wirtschaftsjurist* or a Bachelor of Laws degree. Some of these graduates might be interested in doing a master's degree in law at an English-speaking law school. Admission to a *Fachhochschule* is not limited to those pupils with the *Abitur* and, as a result, it is said that the quality is not generally as high as at a university. It is also said that, lacking the *Abitur*, the *Wirtschaftsjurist* is not likely to posses the same knowledge of foreign languages as the university student. This being said, as mentioned below, some universities are already granting a bachelor's degree after only two years of study, often with a curriculum that is quite similar to that offered at *Fachhochschulen*. Although there might be significant differences, at least in general, between the students attending law programs at *Fachhochschulen* and at universities, the curricular differences between these two educational institutions appear to be relatively minor at the Bachelor's level.

University Legal Education

Legal education at a German university depends somewhat on the state in which the university is located and to an even greater extent on the university itself. Nevertheless, every law student in Germany begins with general law studies. Although these general law studies are designed to be completed in four semesters, some 80% of the students in Münster complete their coursework in three. Students write an examination in each class and the grades are collected and averaged into a GPA on the so-called *Zwischenprüfung*, meaning intermediate examination, but not actually administered as an examination but rather as a compilation of the grades earned in individual classes. A few universities confer the degree of LLB upon completion of the *Zwischenprüfung*. After the *Zwischenprüfung* comes the so-called *Schwerpunktbereich*, or area of specialisation, which encompasses two semesters. Here one finds some variation among the universities in the areas of specialisation. Münster offers the following areas of specialisation: international law, European law, and international private law (conflicts of law); employment and social welfare law; civil procedure and dispute resolution; media, telecommunications, and internet law; tax law; constitutional and administrative law; criminal law; business and company law. As with the *Zwischenprüfung*, the *Schwerpunktbereich* also ends with a certificate which lists the courses and gives the GPA, often together with the student's relative standing in his or her area of specialization. As discussed below, the grade in the area of specialization becomes part of the grade in the first state examination. After completing the *Schwerpunktbereich*, almost all students spend two additional semesters preparing for the first state examination, as discussed below under *Repetitorium*. Those who pass the first state examination are admitted to the public service internship, lasting two years (*Referendariat*) and ending with the second examination, which qualifies them to be hired as a civil servant, including as a judge.

University legal education in Germany is often described as one intended to train judges and other civil servants, not lawyers. The instruction is also closely affiliated with legal positivistic thinking, specifically with the idea that law is "made" (it has a pedigree) by the legislature. Law is almost always identified with power (the so-called *Machtmonopol des Staates*) and, typical for legal positivism, morality is not ordinarily an issue. The law student endeavors to find what the law is and to apply that law correctly; he or she is much less concerned about what may or may not be reasonable under the circumstances.

Law teaching at a university in Germany is, in a word, academic, set in a historical and systematic framework. Great emphasis is placed on legal vocabulary and on broad, abstract statements of the law. Cases are regularly discussed in class, but they are classic cases used to illustrate that there is a right answer to (most) legal questions. Law is seldom questioned, nor its consequences discussed; rather, it is applied. It might be said that the purpose of the German legal education is to train humanistic, "scientifically" trained, conscientious civil servants.

The classes in the area of general law studies (*Zwischenprüfung*) are offered in criminal, public, and private law, generally in a ratio of 1:2:3 reflecting their relative weight in the state examination (see below). While an examination is written in each class, the grade has little significance for it does not become part of one's overall GPA. Some students spend a semester abroad, usually on the ERASMUS-Socrates program, but in recent years the number of students doing so has been declining. One class in "soft skills" (*Schlüsselqualifikationen*) is required. This requirement can be met by taking a class in debating, negotiation, public speaking, or something of the like. In addition, every student must pass one foreign law class, taught in a foreign language, or a law-based foreign language class. At Münster, for example, this requirement can be met by taking a class in Russian Law, Common Law, French Law, Spanish Law, or Turkish Law.

In the areas of specialization students must write a term paper, usually written in conjunction with a seminar. An examination is given at the end of each class and the accumulated grade makes up 30% of the grade on the first state examination (see below). Despite the Bologna process, no university degree is ordinarily given upon completion, although there are a few universities in Germany which give their students a Bachelor of Laws degree at this juncture. In the state of North Rhine-Westphalia, where Münster is located, there are five universities (Bielefeld, Bochum, Bonn, Düsseldorf, and Münster) who award the degree *Diplomjurist* to their students, but only after they have passed the first state examination.

The Bucerius Law School, the only private law school in Germany, opened its doors in Hamburg in the year 2000. Bucerius Law School is one of the law faculties that award their students a Bachelor of Laws degree after three years of study. The law school sets its own enrollment at 110 students a year, far smaller than the six to seven hundred enrolled annually at the University of Münster. Bucerius also uses a written and an oral examination to select students from a large applicant pool. The curriculum is divided into ten terms

(*Trimester*), one of which must be spent at an English-language law school. Bucerius also require two, three-month internships, and they provide their students with two terms of preparation for the first state examination. According to reports, most of the students who graduate from Bucerius also end up going to a private *Repetitor* (see below). The cost of this education is presently EUR39,600 or USD51,360 at the present exchange rate. Despite the high fees, Bucerius boasts that they have six applicants for every place in their entering class. Their students have also done extremely well on the first state exam (see below).

Before leaving the subject of university education, a few words should be said about the doctorate in law, *Dr. jur.*, which is awarded by law faculties, including the Bucerius Law School, but not by *Fachhochschulen*. Although some universities are more lenient than others, most universities require a grade of *Prädikat* (see discussion below on first state examination) on the first state examination to be accepted as a doctoral candidate. The doctoral candidate presents herself or himself to a professor and agrees to a dissertation topic which is generally discussed in a dissertation covering 150–250 pages in length. No additional coursework is required. Although doctoral candidates sometimes complete their dissertations in six months, it is more common to spend a year, sometimes longer, depending on whether the doctoral candidate is working part-time. The mode is probably one and a half years.

Upon completion, the dissertation is submitted to the doctoral adviser who writes a review and recommends a grade of summa cum laude, magna cum laude, cum laude, or rite. The dissertation and the written analysis of the doctoral advisor are passed on to a second professor, who ordinarily agrees with the assessment of the doctoral advisor. There is no evaluation outside the university. The process ends either, as in Münster, with an oral exam on general German law (*Rigorosum*) or, particularly at small faculties, with a public defense of the dissertation. This step is basically a formality since no one has ever failed the *Rigorosum* or the defense; however, performance in the *Rigorosum* or defense may influence the overall grade. To give the reader some idea of the prevalence of doctorates in Germany, the University of Münster ordinarily awards 100 doctorates annually, although one year it awarded 150. As there are usually over 600 students from Münster who pass the first state exam annually, and since most of the doctoral students will write their dissertations at their home universities, one can conclude that about one in six law graduates, at most, will obtain a doctorate. Munich, which has approximately the same size student body as Münster, awards only 50 doctorates annually.

Study of foreign law

As mentioned above, all German law students are required to take either a law class taught in a foreign language or a foreign language class that introduces students to foreign legal terminology. The grade is, however, of no consequence. That is not the case for the foreign law programs offered by various universities. Most universities style their program a *fachspezifische Fremdsprachenausbildung*, literally a subject-specific foreign-language course, although one program, that in Jena, is called simply Language and Law. The programs vary dramatically in what they require, with Münster being the most demanding. Münster offers the foreign law program in three languages: English (Common Law), French, and Spanish. To be admitted, students take a computer-based test in which they are presented with three texts in their chosen language in which letters have been removed from individual words. The test-taker's task is to insert the correct letter or letters into the gaps in the texts. A perfect score of 100 is said to be comparable to the skill level of a native speaker. For admission to the foreign law program in Münster, the student must score 70%. According to the language center of the University of Münster, a score of 70% on the computer-based test in Münster, called the C-test, is equivalent to a score of 600 on the written TOEFL, 250 on the computer-based TOEFL, and 100 on the internet TOEFL.

To complete the foreign law program in Münster, the 200 students admitted annually must take five law classes and four language classes of two classroom hours weekly over a period of four semesters. The law classes, all of which are taught by native English-speaking lawyers, judges, and academics, are the Common Law Legal System, the Common Law of Torts, the Common Law of Contract, Constitutional Law (either British, American, or Australian), and an elective. At present Münster offers as electives courses in the Law of War, Recent Constitutional Developments in the UK and EU, International Business Transactions, International Dispute Resolution, and Company Law. At present, the lecturers include partners from leading global law firms, judges from Australia, from the U.S. federal court, from the European Court of Justice, and from the House of Lords, and professors from the London School of Economics, the University of the West of England, Norwich Law School, Suffolk Law School, Roger Williams University, the University of Lancaster, and the University of Virginia. The classes at the language center, some of which are taught by native English-speakers and some of which, such as legal translating, are taught by Germans, are: Legal Research and Writing, Legal

Translating, Skills for Law (Common Law Legal System), and Conversation and Presentation Skills for Lawyers. In addition, every student must satisfactorily complete a three-week internship in an English-speaking law environment and pass an oral examination. The oral examination and the courses are all graded, so that upon graduation from the program, the student receives a certificate in foreign law with a GPA.

Until recently, it was neither possible nor common for German lawyers to do a Master of Laws degree in Germany; the masters programs at German universities were limited to foreign students. After the introduction of tuition fees, of EUR 2,200 annually, the number of foreign students on the LLM course at the University of Münster dropped to about 30. Many of these foreign students hope to be able to write a dissertation, which is possible if they do very well on the LLM course. For the German students, of the 600 or so students from Münster who pass the first state exam each year, 50 to 100 attend an LLM program, almost all in a common law country. In addition, many German students from other universities are coming to Münster to attend one of three LLM programs offered in Mergers and Acquisitions, Real Estate Law, and International Taxation. The tuition fees for these LLM programs average around EUR14,000 per year.

In 2005 Münster hosted the LLM Fair Europe, the first of its kind in the world. In its initial year, representatives of over 30 international law schools presented their LLM and other academic programs to students from Münster and surrounding universities. In the years since, Münster has limited the number of universities at the fair to ten. In making its selection, Münster considers, among other factors, the location of the university, its reputation for scholarship and teaching, and cost. Through the years, Münster has developed good working relationships with a number of foreign law schools, including the Norwich Law School and the University of the West of England in England, Suffolk University Law School in Boston, the University of Virginia, the University of Connecticut, California Western School of Law in San Diego, La Trobe University in Australia, and the University of Auckland in New Zealand. All of these law schools have cooperated in providing Münster with the criteria that they use in selecting students to enable staff of Münster's LLM Center to pre-select students for recommendation to their programs. Most of the universities have also established scholarship programs, enticing excellent students from Münster and elsewhere in Germany to study there. Münster is always looking for new partners among universities that meet the high standards and conditions of those universities with which it has an on-going relationship.

First State Examination

The first state examination is administered by the judicial examination offices (*Justizprüfungsämter*). In order to be admitted to take the examination, the law graduate must present his or her certificate from the *Schwerpunktbereich*, or area of specialization, as well as documentation showing that he or she has completed two, six-week internships, one with a lawyer and one with an administrative agency. The examination itself consists of six written factual situations for the student to discuss: three from private law, two from public law, and one from criminal law. After the written essays have been graded, the students are invited in groups of four to six to be examined by three examiners. Those grading the written examinations and conducting the oral examinations are, in most cases, judges and public prosecutors. All university law professors, and a small number of attorneys, also take part in the examinations, although not always on a regular basis, meaning that the vast majority of examiners are judges and public prosecutors.

The essays and the oral examination are graded on a scale of zero to eighteen, with eighteen being the best. Those who score an average of 9.0 to 18.0 points are said to have a *Prädikatsexamen.* Those scoring 9.0 and above are considered "fully satisfactory". Those scoring 11.5 and above are given the score "good", and those scoring 14.0 and above are awarded the grade "very good". There is also the grade of satisfactory (6.0 to 8.99 points) and passing (4.0 to 6.49 points). Passage rates vary widely by university. For example, in Saxony, 59% of the test-takers pass the examination, in Münster 90% of the students pass the examination, and at the Bucerius Law School 100% of the students pass the examination. The average passage rate for all of Germany is 72%. In other words, 28% of those who take the first state exam fail the exam. If they fail, they are generally allowed two further attempts. Thus, in part because of the high failure rate, only 10,000 students out of the 21,000 who started their studies of law actually finish them by passing the first state examination.

The percentage of *Prädikatsexamen* also varies by university and by *Bundesland* (state), with the *Bundesland* Sachsen-Anhalt having the lowest percentage (13%) and the *Bundesland* Hamburg having the highest percentage

(37%). The average for all of Germany is 22%, but a number of law schools have rates in excess of this. In Münster, for example, 25% of the students earn a *Prädikatsexamen* and at the Bucerius Law School the percentage is 96%.

Before sitting the first state exam, almost all students, including those from the Bucerius Law School, take courses taught by a *Repetitor* to help them prepare for the examination. In effect, therefore, going to a *Repetitor* is practically obligatory. The *Repetitorium* is offered by unregulated private companies that teach the students black letter law and exam-writing. Although many law faculties, such as at the University of Münster, offer these courses as well, the courses taught by the universities attract very few students, and usually those students they do attract are also enrolled with a private company. Most students go a *Repetitor* for one year, although some start in their first semester and continue all the way through. Students spend for this instruction anywhere from EUR2,600 to over EUR4,000 for a one-year course and materials.

Referendariat

A student who passes the first state examination is entitled to be employed by the state as an intern at approximately EUR10,800 (USD14,000 at the present exchange rate) annually. During this two-year internship (*Referendariat*), the stagiaries (*Referendare*, plural form) are supervised by the judicial examination offices as they pass through the so-called stages of their training. The first stage is at the civil court (4 months), then comes the criminal court or prosecutor (4 months), then an administrative agency (4 months), then a private attorney (9 months), and finally an elective, or *Wahlstation* (3 months). While the *Referendar* is working for a court or private attorney, he or she must attend tutorials, usually taught weekly by judges, in preparation for the second state examination.

Second State Examination

The second examination consists of eight written essay examinations based on factual situations, but it stresses procedural law rather than the substantive law tested in the first state examination. There is also an oral examination which includes analysis of a case file. At this point of one's legal education, it is practically impossible to fail. If one fails the examination, he or she is allowed to retake it. If he or she fails again, a judge is personally assigned to the person to make sure that he or she passes on the third attempt. Upon passage of the second state examination, the *Referendar* is allowed to refer to himself as *Assessor.*

Summary of Recent Developments in Legal Education

There are three major developments in legal education that can be seen in the above discussion. First there are certain structural changes: a movement from being selective to being competitive in the school system, also the introduction of tuition fees, although it is uncertain how these fees will be spent. Tuition fees in law are likely to equal approximately EUR300 per semester. Many administrators are concerned that if they use these funds to employ more teaching staff, the courts will just allocate more students to them, negating any beneficial effect. There is also political pressure on the universities to bring their curriculum in line with the *Fachhochschulen*, particularly by granting the students a bachelor of laws degree after the completion of two and a half to three years of study. One also sees more differentiation between universities as they vie to attract students.

There are also curricular changes, particularly the requirement to take classes in foreign law and language and in 'soft skills'. The specialization is also new, and reflects the policy of speeding up the legal education and providing the students with a marketable specialization upon their graduation. The instruction at the university still emphasizes the education of civil servants, and this is also the case with instruction during the *Referendariat.*

The third development is a movement toward internationalization. There is more interest in European and international law, especially international commercial law, and there has been an increase in foreign, minority students studying in Germany, although many of them now have obtained German citizenship. There is also an increased interest in public international law, particularly human rights. And, most importantly for purposes of this LLM guide, there has been a large increase in the interest of students in studying abroad, particularly in common law countries.

Authors

Ruth Bader Ginsburg, Justice, U.S. Supreme Court, One First Street N.E.,Washington, DC.

Stephen C. Hicks, Professor of Law, Suffolk University Law School, Boston, MA, shicks@suffolk.edu

Thomas Lundmark, Professor, Dr.iur., Faculty of Law, Westphalian Wilhelm's University of Münster, Münster, Germany
thlund@uni-muenster.de

Kjell Å. Modéer, Professor emeritus of Legal history, Faculty of Law, Lund University, Lund, Sweden
Kjell_A.Modeer@jur.lu.se

Mathias W. Reimann, Hessel E. Yntema Professor of Law, University of Michigan Law School, Ann Arbor, MI.
purzel@umich.edu

Michael L. Rustad, Thomas F. Lambert Jr. Professor of Law, Suffolk University Law School, Boston, MA.
mrustad@suffolk.edu

John Henry Schlegel, Professor of Law, Roger and Karen Jones Faculty Scholar, University at Buffalo Law School, The State University of New York, Buffalo, NY.
schlegel@acsu.buffalo.edu

Bruce P. Smith, Dean and Guy Raymond Jones Faculty Scholar, University of Illinois College of Law, Champaign, IL.
smithb@illinois.edu